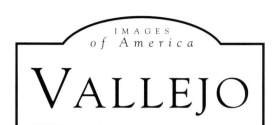

IMAGES
of America

VALLEJO

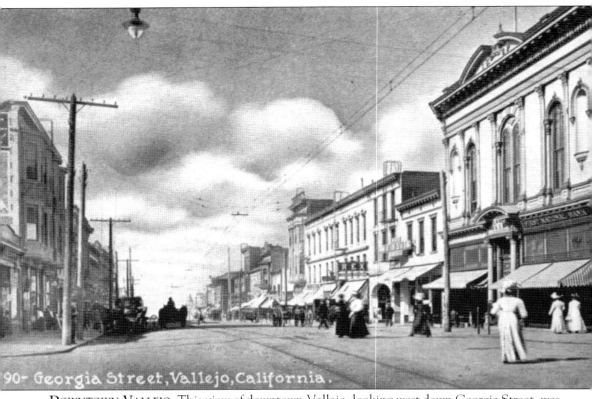

90- Georgia Street, Vallejo, California.

DOWNTOWN VALLEJO. This view of downtown Vallejo, looking west down Georgia Street, was taken around 1910. The lines overhead powered electric trains that carried passengers from the ferry wharf at the foot of Georgia Street north to towns in the Napa Valley. At right is the Oddfellow's Hall at the corner of Georgia and Marin Streets.

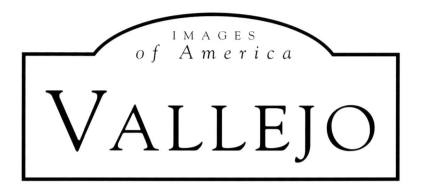

IMAGES
of America

VALLEJO

James E. Kern

ARCADIA

Published by Arcadia Publishing
Charleston SC, Chicago IL, Portsmouth NH, San Francisco CA

Printed in the United States of America

Library of Congress Catalog Card Number: 2004106995

For all general information contact Arcadia Publishing at:
Telephone 843-853-2070
Fax 843-853-0044
E-mail sales@arcadiapublishing.com
For customer service and orders:
Toll-Free 1-888-313-2665

Visit us on the Internet at www.arcadiapublishing.com

CONTENTS

ACKNOWLEDGMENTS

Since the Vallejo Naval and Historical Museum was founded in 1974, hundreds of volunteers have contributed tens of thousands of hours to preserve the history of Vallejo and Mare Island. It is impossible to thank all of those volunteers individually, but without their hard work and their love of local history this book would not have been possible. The Vallejo Museum's research library, archives, and photo collections offer a treasure trove of fascinating stories and information about the community's history. The staff members and volunteers who maintain these collections have earned my immeasurable gratitude.

I also wish to thank my editor at Arcadia Publishing, Hannah Clayborn, for her expert guidance (when requested) and prodding (when needed). Also, Mrs. Janet Topley who generously granted permission to reproduce images from the Vallejo Museum's Topley Photo Collection, and publisher Ron Rhea and editor Ted Vollmer of the Vallejo *Times-Herald* who provided unlimited access to that newspaper's extensive photo archives.

There are several people who have paved the way for this book through their research, writing, and enthusiasm for local history. Specifically, I wish to thank Lee Fountain, Matthew Fountain, Sue Lemmon, Thomas Lucy, Midge Lund, and Ernest Wichels for their many contributions toward preserving our community's history.

Dr. Eric Cardinal, Harry F. Lupold, and Judy Furlong provided the early guidance and encouragement that fostered my interest in local history and that ultimately led to this book. Finally to my wife, Chris, thank you for your love and encouragement, not just on this project, but in everything.

INTRODUCTION

Vallejo has always been a "crossroads community," a city of transitions. The earliest inhabitants of the region traveled through the area where the city of Vallejo is now located, but for the most part they did not stay. The Suscol Native American tribe to the north, the Suisun tribe to the east, and the Karkins, who lived along the straits that later would bear their name, all came to this area to gather tules to build their homes, hunt in the grass-covered hills, and fish in the abundance of the bay. But usually they returned to larger nearby villages and did not settle here permanently.

Europeans first came in the 1770s, but they too were just passing through. Members of an expedition led by Lieutenant Pedro Fages first saw the straits, the lush green hillsides, and the long, low island at the mouth of the Napa River in March 1772. Three years later, Jose Canizares, a member of the de Anza Expedition, drew the first map of the area and called the island *Isla Plana*—the flat island. But these were explorers, not settlers, and they continued on their way.

In 1833 a young *Californio* named Mariano Guadalupe Vallejo passed through the area on his way to Sonoma, where he would take up the post of *commandante* of Mexico's northern frontier. General Vallejo obtained several large Mexican land grants and one of them, the *Rancho Suscol*, included the land where the cities of Vallejo and Benicia would later be built. Vallejo raised cattle for hides and tallow, and maintained a small garrison of troops at the Sonoma Barracks. Transportation was usually on foot, by horse or by boat. A popular story holds that Vallejo was transporting horses on a boat across the Carquinez Straits one day when the vessel capsized and the horses were swept into the water. Vallejo's favorite horse, a white mare, swam ashore on the *Isla Plana* and, after she was rescued, the island gained a new name: *Isla de la Yegua,* or Island of the Mare.

As Vallejo advanced his career and increased his power in northern California, he became more and more convinced that Californians would best be served if they annexed themselves to the United States. Mexico was losing its tenuous grip on the northern frontier, and General Vallejo realized that the westward-expanding American empire would eventually reach California, and that Californians had better be ready for its arrival.

But events moved more rapidly than even Vallejo could anticipate. The Bear Flag Revolt in 1846 and the discovery of gold in 1848 changed California dramatically, although the ever-reliant General Vallejo stayed ahead of the game. When California was admitted to the Union in 1850, Vallejo offered 156 acres of his land to the State of California to build a new state capital. General Vallejo proposed that the city be named Eureka, but a grateful state legislature named the new city Vallejo in his honor. In 1852 the state capital moved from San Jose to Vallejo. Now the seat of state government, the town of Vallejo welcomed the state legislature with open arms, but the government officials also would just be passing through. Primitive conditions in the newly-built city forced the legislature to move, first to Benicia and then to Sacramento. Another transition.

In 1854 the U. S. Navy arrived. The navy acquired Mare Island and there they established the first U. S. Naval Base on the Pacific coast. As Mare Island grew, the city of Vallejo grew along with it. But as a maritime port, Vallejo would continue in its role as a "crossroads community." Sailors and their ships came and went. The civilian workforce at Mare Island grew and declined and grew again, reflecting the many vacillations in America's military and political life.

Along with its identity as a navy town, Vallejo also became a center of trade and transportation. The railroad arrived in the 1860s and connected Vallejo with other communities in northern California and, ultimately, with the rest of the United States. Ships of all kind came and went, from scow-schooners transporting goods across the bay, to ferries carrying people between cities, to naval and commercial vessels from the four corners of the world. Within this maritime city, businesses connected to sea-going trade thrived. Lumber was shipped through the Carquinez Straits to build the cities of the growing state of California. Grain was shipped from the fruitful Central Valley where it was milled into flour at Vallejo and then continued on its journey to the cities of Europe, Asia and South America. These many businesses and industries also provided the opportunities for a better life that attracted new residents from across the United States and all around the world. Immigrants from China, Japan, and the Philippines reflected Vallejo's connection with the Pacific Rim. Other immigrants arrived from South and Central America and from European nations like England, Ireland, Germany, Portugal, Italy, Russia, and France. The city became a crossroads for the world.

From its rough-and-tumble pioneer beginnings in the 19th century, Vallejo grew in the 20th century into a diverse and thriving community, supported by the reliable federal payroll at Mare Island. New highways, bridges, civic buildings, and comfortable homes reflected the stability of this solid, mostly blue-collar community. The United States broke out of its isolation and became a player on the world stage. Mare Island grew to support that role, and so too did the City of Vallejo. As America became involved in foreign affairs, Mare Island supplied the ships that supported that involvement. The Spanish-American War and World War I brought growth to the city and the shipyard, but their impact would pale in comparison to the tremendous changes caused by World War II. That tumultuous era brought unprecedented growth to Vallejo and saw the city's population nearly triple. Once again, people from all over the United States came to the "crossroads community" to work at the busy shipyard. Thousands of sailors passed through Mare Island to the Pacific War Zone. Many never returned.

When the war ended, many civilian workers went back to their home states. Others remained in Vallejo and built homes in the new post-war neighborhoods that sprang up east and north of the old part of town. The next transition would come in the early 1960s when city fathers decided to demolish much of old downtown Vallejo and build a new, forward looking town center and civic plaza. Surrounding rural land was annexed and the city continued to grow.

Vallejo faced the challenges and social changes of the 1960s and emerged with its strong sense of community intact. Vallejoans are, and always have been, avid sports fans, supporters of the arts, believers in education, strong in their faith, and have demonstrated the true essence of community spirit. And although they have come to this "crossroads community" from all around the world, and for a variety of different reasons, Vallejoans love their city and continue to work together to make it thrive.

One
CITY BEGINNINGS
1850–1900

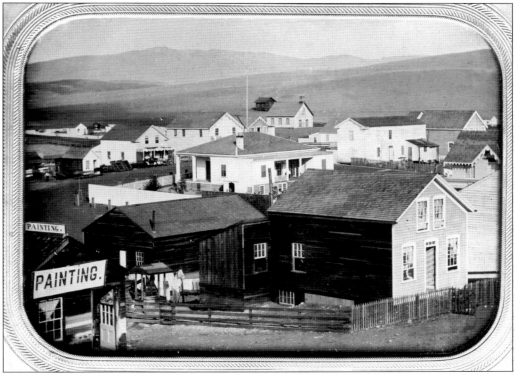

EARLIEST KNOWN PHOTOGRAPH OF VALLEJO. The City of Vallejo played an important role during the early days of California statehood. Founded as the state capital, and soon thereafter the home of the first U. S. Navy Base in the Pacific, Vallejo also had a strategic location on the Carquinez Straits, the gateway to the California gold fields. This early view of the young town of Vallejo was taken around 1857 from the second story of the state capitol building, looking east. In the center of the photo is the home of John Frisbie, Vallejo's founder. Behind Frisbie's home is a two- story building that once housed the offices of the secretary of state. In the background is the Methodist Church, Vallejo's first church, built in 1856.

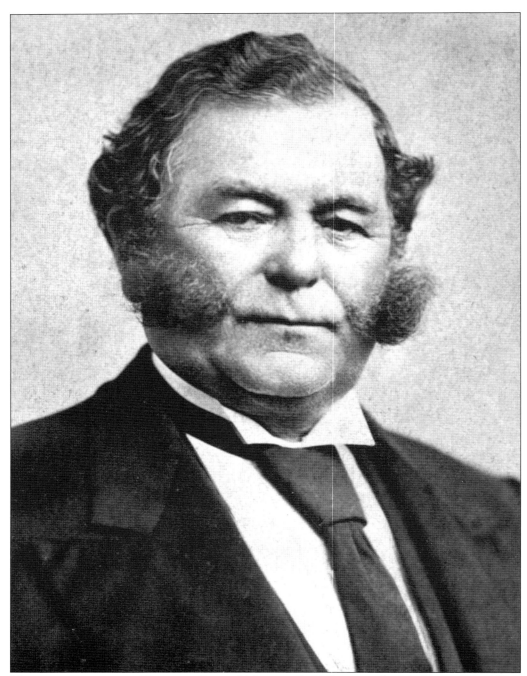

MARIANO GUADALUPE VALLEJO. General Mariano G. Vallejo was the Mexican *commandante* of northern California and owned several large *ranchos*, or land grants. Among these was the *Rancho Suscol*, which included the site of the present-day city of Vallejo. After California was admitted to the Union in 1850, General Vallejo proposed that a new state capital be established, and he donated 156 acres of his land for that purpose. The grateful state legislature named the new city Vallejo in his honor.

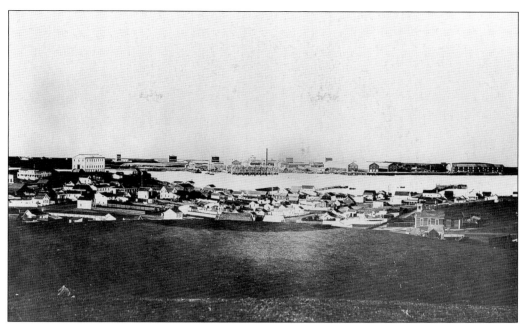

THE STATE CAPITOL BUILDING IN VALLEJO. The California State Legislature convened in Vallejo for the first time on January 5, 1852. A new capitol building, shown here at left, had been erected on a hill near the corner of York and Sacramento Streets. Primitive conditions in the young city of Vallejo forced the legislature to flee after just one week. The state government returned to Vallejo in January 1853 but conditions had improved very little, so the legislature relocated to Benicia. After the departure of the state government, the former capitol building became a warehouse. It was destroyed by fire in August 1859.

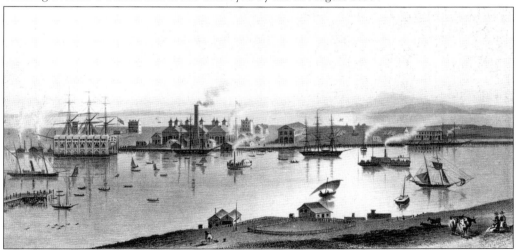

MARE ISLAND NAVY YARD. Following the departure of the state legislature the town of Vallejo fell on hard times. The city was nearly depopulated and many of the original structures were torn down or moved. However, in 1854, Captain David Farragut arrived at Mare Island to establish the first U.S. Navy Yard on the Pacific Coast. The founding of Mare Island marked the start of a 142-year relationship between the U.S. Navy and the City of Vallejo. Vallejo established its identity as a "navy town."

11

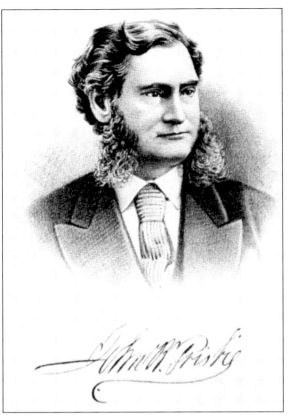

VALLEJO'S FOUNDING FAMILY. John B. Frisbie was married to Mariano Vallejo's oldest daughter, Epifania, also known as Fannie. After the City of Vallejo was designated California's state capital, Frisbie commissioned the survey to lay out the city's streets. He promoted the city among early settlers and generously donated land for the construction of churches, a public school, and a city park. He was one of the founders of Vallejo's first bank and was instrumental in convincing the federal government to purchase Mare Island.

FRISBIE FAMILY HOMES. John and Fannie Frisbie's first two homes are shown here. The single-story house at left was the family's first home, built prior to 1856. The two-story brick house was the Frisbie's second home in Vallejo. The location is the southeast corner of Georgia and Sacramento Streets. Both of these buildings were later moved to York Street when the Bernard House and Levee's Department store were built.

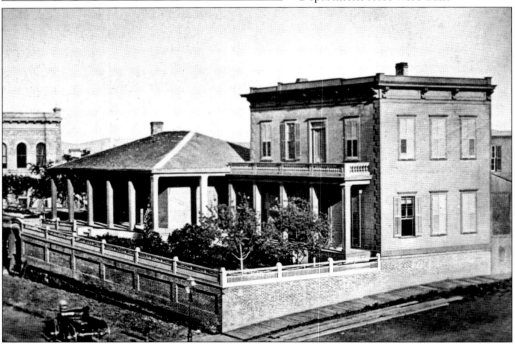

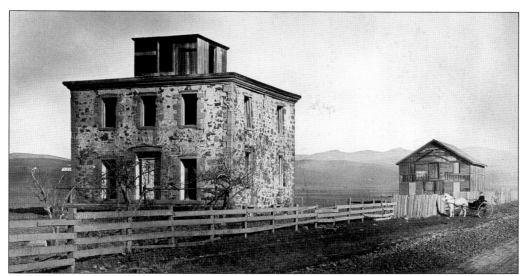

The Old Stone House. This interesting residence, known as the "Old Stone House," was the home of Manuel Vierra and was probably built in the 1850s. In 1863, Vierra shot a squatter who had illegally settled on his land. Vierra was arrested and confined in a boarding house on Georgia Street while officials deliberated whether charges should be brought against him. On May 6, 1863, a group of vigilantes rode into town, dragged Vierra into the street, and murdered him. The killers were never prosecuted.

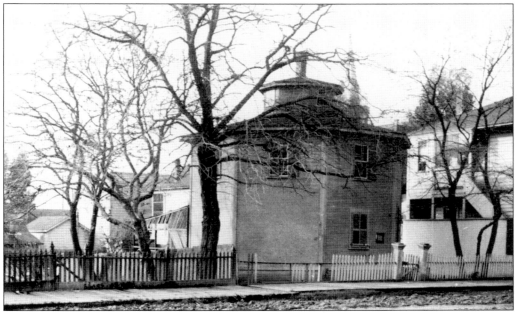

THE "INK BOTTLE" HOUSE. Vallejo's octagonal "Ink Bottle" House stood on the south side of Florida Street, between Marin Street and Sonoma Boulevard. According to the Vallejo *Times-Herald* in 1936, the unusual house was built around 1865 by "an eccentric sea captain whose name even the old timers have forgotten." In later years, the Daley and Colton families lived in the house. The octagon was torn down around 1908, though some accounts have it standing, abandoned, into the 1910s.

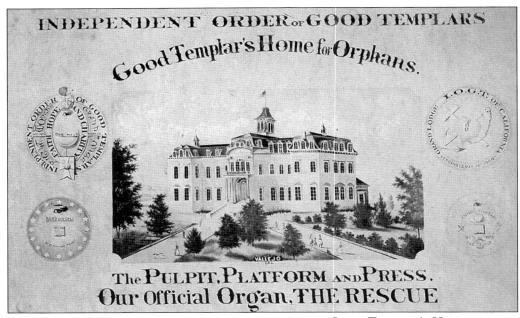

INDEPENDENT ORDER of GOOD TEMPLARS

Good Templar's Home for Orphans.

VALLEJO

The PULPIT, PLATFORM and PRESS.

Our Official Organ, THE RESCUE

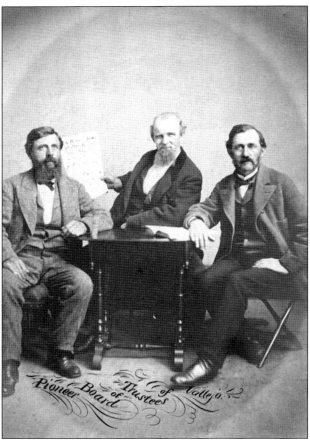

Pioneer Board of Trustees of Vallejo.

GOOD TEMPLAR'S HOME FOR ORPHANS. From 1869 to 1922 the Good Templar's Home for Orphans provided care for needy children from throughout California. Despite many years of outstanding public service, the home ultimately closed after a scandal involving murder and sexual abuse. The grounds of the home later served as the Vallejo Municipal Golf Course. In the 1930s the Vista de Vallejo subdivision was built on the hilltop location.

VALLEJO'S PIONEER BOARD OF TRUSTEES. From 1851 to 1867 the town of Vallejo was governed by a justice of the peace and a town constable. When Vallejo was incorporated as a city in 1867, the government changed to an elected body of three city trustees. From 1868 to 1872 the trustees leased offices at the Washington Hotel on Georgia Street for $25 a month. The first trustees, from left to right, were Eben Hilton, William Greeves, and William Aspenall.

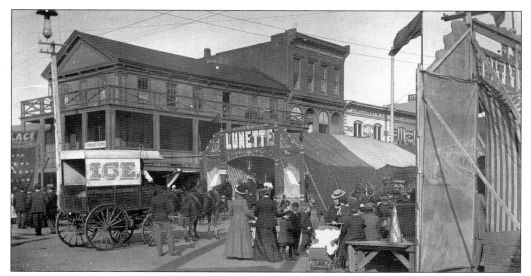

A Celebration on Georgia Street. Vallejoans enjoy a street fair at the corner of Georgia and Sacramento Streets in this photo. The building in the background was known as the Colby Block. At various times it contained an upholstery shop, meat market, grocery store, saloon, notions store, millinery shop, and more. According to one account, the lumber used to build the Colby Block came from the State of Maine and was brought around Cape Horn by ship. The building was probably built in the early 1860s.

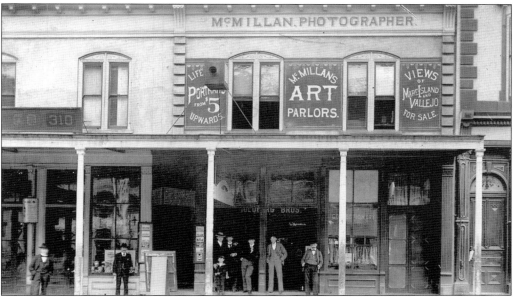

McMillan Photo Studio. Charles McMillan operated Vallejo's leading photographic studio at the turn of the last century. His Solano Art Studio, shown here in 1895, was located at 314 Georgia Street. McMillan was born in Canada and began his career as a photographer in Chicago, then moved to California in 1879. He traveled the state, operating his photo studio out of a tent, before eventually settling in Vallejo. Other early Vallejo photographers included J. G. Smith, W. F. Henry, A. J. Perkins, E. K. Halverson, J. C. Parsons, and members of the Topley family.

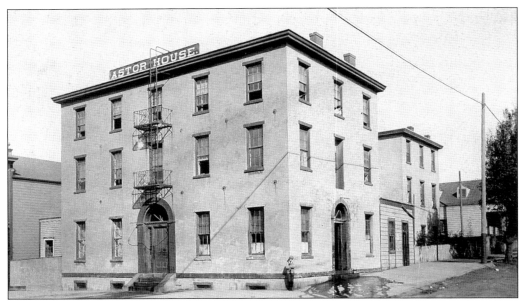

THE ASTOR HOUSE. The popular Astor House was a hotel and restaurant built in the 1850s. Originally called the Metropolitan Hotel, it was located at the corner of Virginia and Santa Clara Streets. After the Civil War, proprietor George Voorhees renamed the hotel the Sherman House in honor of Civil War General William T. Sherman. A later proprietor, William Tormey, gave it the name Astor House. The Virginia Street landmark was torn down in the early 1960s.

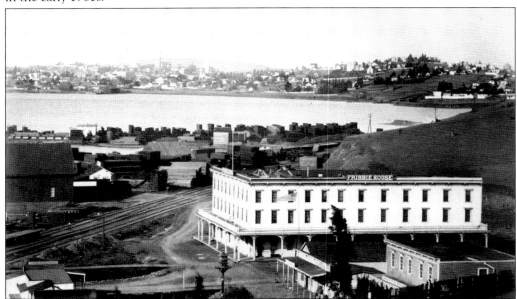

THE FRISBIE HOUSE. During the mid-19th century, South Vallejo grew as a center of commerce and transportation. In the 1880s author Robert Louis Stevenson and his new bride stayed at the Frisbie House hotel in South Vallejo on their way to their honeymoon in Calistoga. Stevenson would later write about his brief stay in Vallejo in his book *The Silverado Squatters*. Unfortunately, the author was not very impressed with Vallejo. He described it as "a blunder."

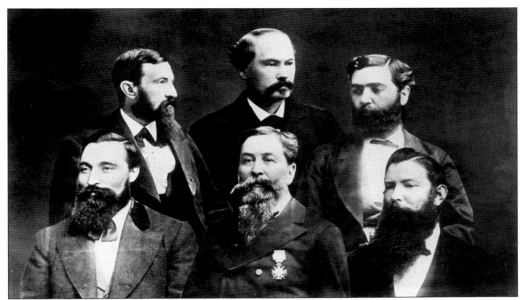

SIX PIONEER PHYSICIANS. Among Vallejo's medical pioneers were Dr. Levi Frisbie, the city's first physician and brother of city founder John Frisbie, and Dr. Platon Vallejo, a son of Mariano G. Vallejo and California's first native-born medical doctor. Other early physicians came to Vallejo through their association with Mare Island and the U.S. Navy. Pictured here, from left to right, are: (front row) Dr. Walter Anderson, Dr. J. M. Browne, and Dr. James Frost; (back row) Dr. William Taylor, Dr. Levi Frisbie, and Dr. Platon Vallejo.

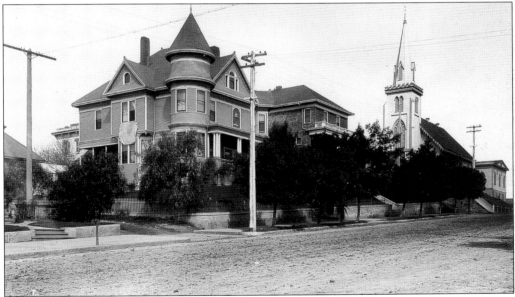

HOME AND OFFICE OF DR. RACHEL LAIN. The turreted Victorian home in the center of this photo was the residence and office of Dr. Rachel Lain, one of Vallejo's earliest women physicians. Dr. Lain was born in Pennsylvania in 1863 and came to California in the 1880s. She established her medical practice in Vallejo in 1891 and died there in 1918. To the right is the First Presbyterian Church, at the corner of Carolina and Marin Streets.

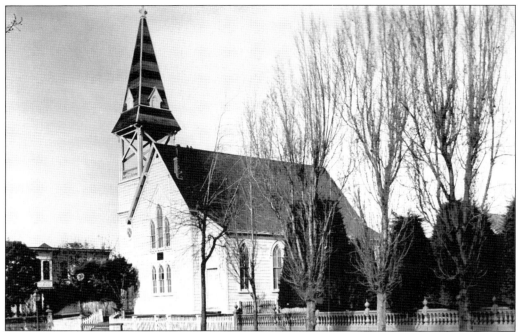

VALLEJO'S FIRST CHURCH. The first church in Vallejo was the Vallejo Methodist Episcopal Church started by Mare Island's founder, David Farragut, his wife, Virginia, and others. In January 1856 John Frisbie donated land on the north side of Virginia Street, between Sonoma Boulevard and Marin Street, for construction of the church. The church building shown here replaced the original church, which was destroyed by fire on October 8, 1878.

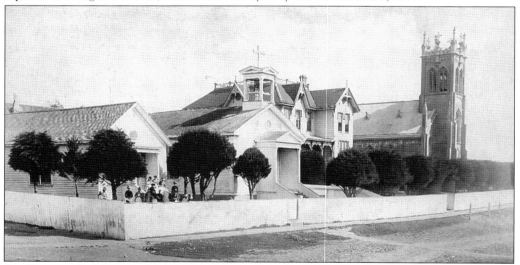

ST. VINCENT'S CATHOLIC CHURCH. The imposing brick edifice of St. Vincent Ferrer Catholic Church has been both a physical and spiritual landmark in Vallejo for many years. Vallejo's first Catholic church was a small wooden structure built in 1855 near the corner of Capitol and Marin Streets. Work on a new brick church began in 1867 on Florida Street. This photo shows the brick church (right) along with the original wooden church, which was moved to the new site from Marin Street.

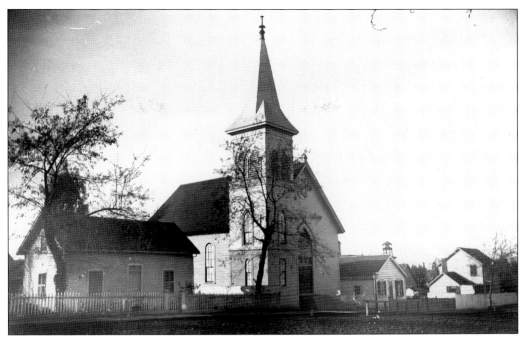

CORNELL BAPTIST CHURCH. The first Baptist church in Vallejo was established by Rev. W. W. Hickie. After meeting in several temporary locations, the congregation purchased a lot on the south side of Marin Street, between Capitol Street and Sonoma Boulevard in 1873. Their church, built at a cost of $5,000, was dedicated on March 1, 1873. The building was extensively remodeled in 1880.

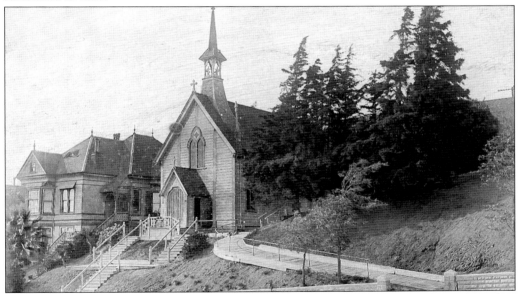

ASCENSION EPISCOPAL CHURCH. In 1867 Vallejo's founder, John B. Frisbie, donated two lots in the 600 block of Georgia Street for the construction of the Ascension Episcopal Church. The cornerstone was laid the next year and the church was officially dedicated on March 13, 1870. The landmark church was destroyed by fire in July 1969.

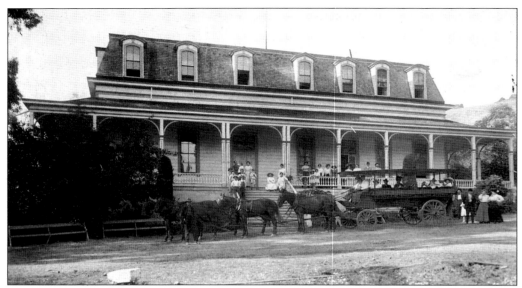

WHITE SULPHUR SPRINGS HOTEL. In 1870 John Frisbie, owner of the White Sulphur Springs, hired architect Amos Petit of Santa Rosa to build a hotel at the popular local resort. Petit was the same contractor hired by Frisbie's father-in-law, Mariano G. Vallejo, to build the state capitol building in Vallejo. The medicinal springs were a popular destination for those seeking health and recreation. White Sulphur Springs is now known as Blue Rock Springs. The hotel was demolished some time in the late 1920s.

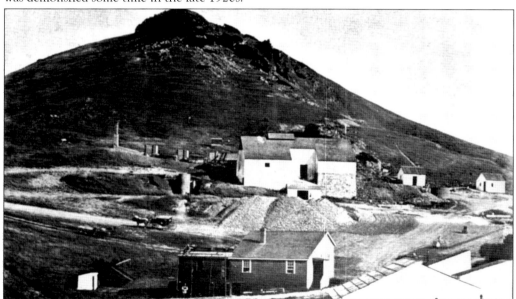

ST. JOHN'S MINE. The St. John's Quicksilver Mining Company was incorporated in April 1873. The Sulphur Springs Mountains surrounding Vallejo were rich in cinnabar ore, from which quicksilver, or mercury, was derived. Mercury was an important part of the gold refining process during California's boisterous Gold Rush era. At its peak, the area around the mine included a blacksmith's shop, mine superintendent's office, furnaceman's house, three workers' dwellings, and a dining hall. The St. John's Mine closed in 1923.

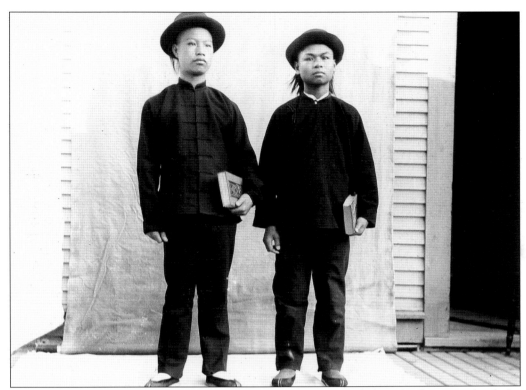

CHINESE IN VALLEJO. Vallejo's Chinese community expanded with the arrival of the California Pacific Railroad in the 1860s. In addition to working on the railroad, the Chinese in Vallejo also found work in local fish canneries, a broom factory, several laundries, restaurants, and as domestic workers employed by local families. By the turn of the 20th century, Mare Island began to open some jobs to Chinese workers, although Chinese opportunities in skilled trades at the shipyard would not be accessible until World War II.

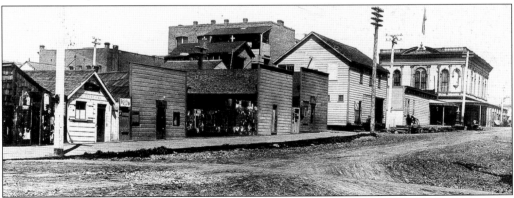

VALLEJO'S CHINATOWN. During the 19th century Vallejo's Chinatown grew up along Marin Street, between Georgia and York Streets. The neighborhood included homes, numerous businesses, meeting halls, and a school. Sing Lee & Company, a clothing manufacturer located at 207 Georgia Street, was one of Vallejo's largest Chinese-owned businesses. Another prominent member of Vallejo's Chinese business community was Joe Soong, whose Vallejo Dollar Store eventually expanded to become the National Dollar Store chain.

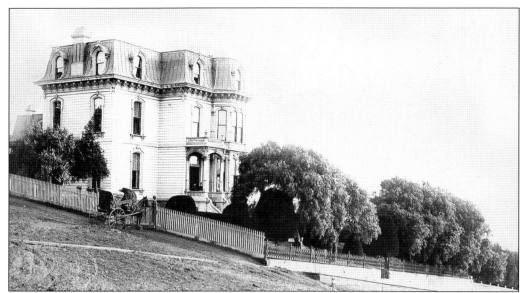

THE FRISBIE'S MANSION ON THE HILL. The third home of Vallejo's founder, General John Frisbie, was located at the corner of Virginia and Sutter Streets. After the Frisbies departed Vallejo, the home was used as a girls' school and, later, as a private residence. Acquired by the Vallejo Elks Lodge in 1920, the building was destroyed in 1933 in a tragic fire that claimed five lives.

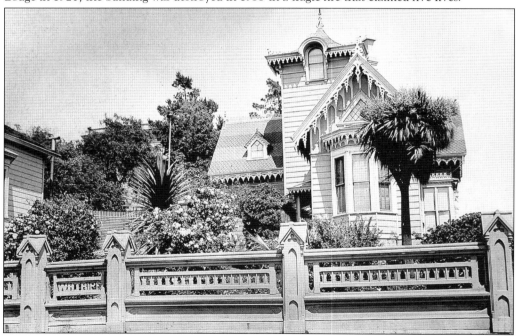

VALLEJO'S ARCHITECTURAL HERITAGE. This Gothic Revival gem, located at 918 Sutter Street, was the home of Prof. William Henry Tripp (1837-1924). In 1867 Tripp opened Tripp's Institute of Penmanship in the Colby Block at the corner of Georgia and Sacramento Streets. Tripp's beautiful home is located in the city's Heritage District, one of several historic neighborhoods in Vallejo that are characterized by a diverse mix of architectural styles.

Two
VALLEJOANS AT WORK

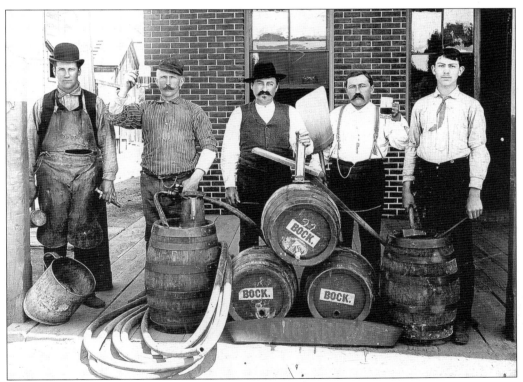

ENJOYING THE FRUITS OF THEIR LABOR. A proud group of workers from Vallejo's Solano Brewery celebrates the tapping of a fresh batch of Spring Bock beer. Pictured, from left to right, are brewery proprietor Charles Widenmann, Chris Bauman, Frank Kleiner, Joe Soans, and an unidentified brewery worker. Like many cities, Vallejo boasted several small breweries in the years prior to Prohibition. Among these were the Solano Brewery on Marin Street, the Pioneer Brewery at the corner of Marin and Carolina Streets, and the Philadelphia Brewery in South Vallejo.

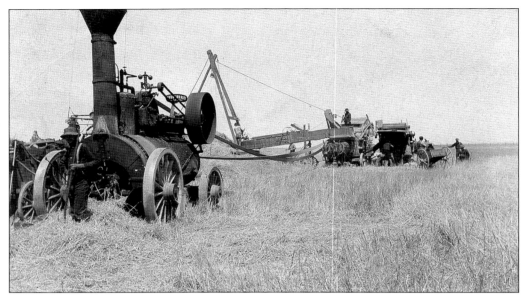

WHEAT THRESHING. A crew harvests wheat at George Rounds's ranch in American Canyon. Rounds later went into the lumber business in Vallejo and in the 1890s served as a member of the city's board of trustees. During Vallejo's pioneer era, the surrounding hills and countryside supported wheat farming, dairy ranches, and other agricultural production.

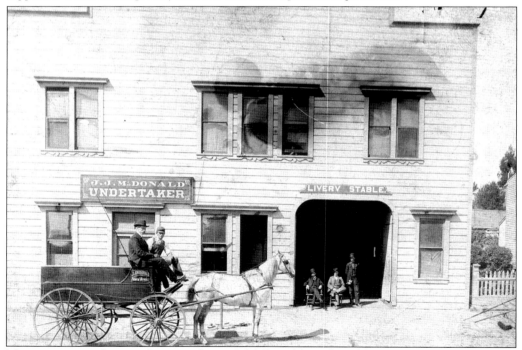

MORTUARY AND LIVERY STABLES. James J. McDonald combined his mortuary business with a livery stable at 216 Virginia Street. McDonald is pictured here on a wagon in front of his business. One of his early ads described the multi-talented McDonald as "undertaker and embalmer, livery and sale stable and county coroner and public administrator."

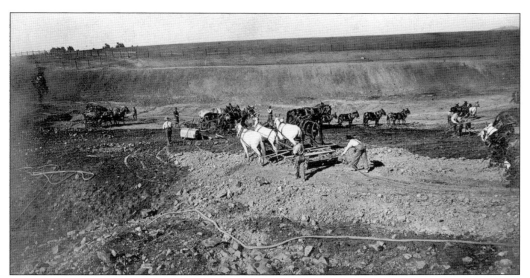

EXCAVATION OF FLEMMING HILL RESERVOIR. In 1911 workers used horse-drawn scoops to excavate a new reservoir on Flemming Hill. Earlier water storage facilities for the city included Lake Chabot and a reservoir at the top of the Capitol Street hill. In the late 19th century several different companies made efforts to develop Vallejo's water system. Eventually the perseverance and hard work of a man named John Frey led to the completion of an extensive and efficient water system. For his efforts, Frey is known as "the Father of Vallejo's Water System."

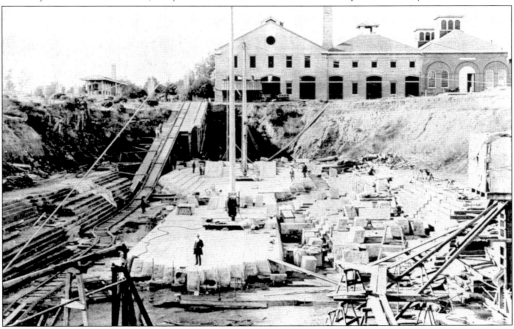

BUILDING THE NAVY YARD. Construction on Mare Island's massive drydock No.1 began in 1878. The huge granite blocks were brought by rail from the Sierra foothills in Placer County, then moved by barge to Mare Island. The final stone in the drydock was set into place on February 18, 1891. Mare Island workers eventually would construct three more of these enormous drydocks.

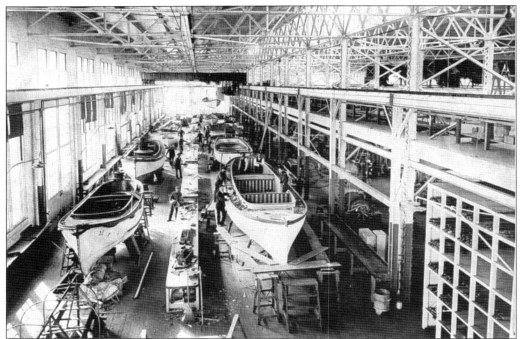

MARE ISLAND'S SMALL BOAT SHOP. Through its long history, the Mare Island Navy Yard built more than 500 ships for the U. S. Navy. Although workers at the shipyard built cruisers, destroyers, submarines, and a battleship, they also built many smaller vessels in the boat shop. Mare Island's small craft were built for the U.S. Navy, but several private boat yards operated in Vallejo as well. Among these were Kimball's Ways, the Vallejo Dock Company, the Standard Launch Company, and Aden Brothers Shipyard.

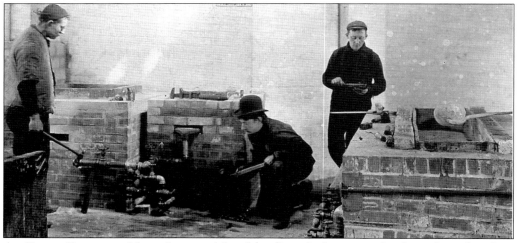

AN EARLY FORGE AT MARE ISLAND. Mare Island's early days were the days of wooden ships and horse-drawn wagons. One of the first buildings completed at the navy yard was a smithy, where workers forged iron fittings for ships, hardware for buildings, shoes for horses, and more. Since it was the only shipyard on the Pacific coast, Mare Island repaired commercial ships and vessels of foreign navies, in addition to U.S. Navy ships. As the navy yard expanded, the young city of Vallejo grew along with it.

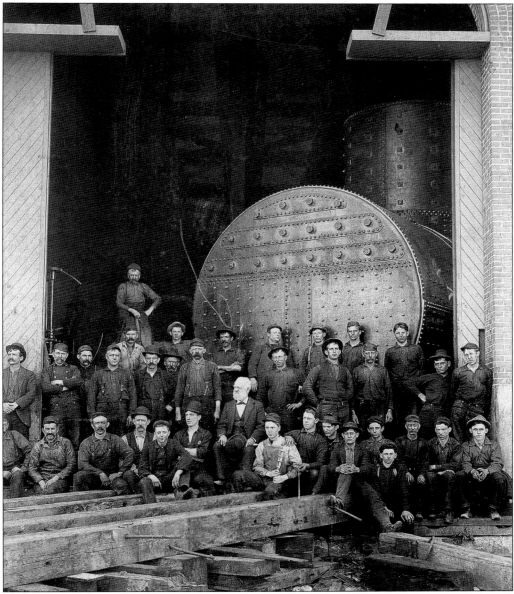

MARE ISLAND'S BOILER SHOP IN 1901. Mare Island grew in importance as a shipbuilding and repair facility following America's naval victories during the Spanish-American War. In July 1901 workers from the navy yard's boiler shop posed for this photo in front of a massive riveted ship's boiler. Shop employees, from left to right, included: (front row) George Boyle, William Kelly, Jackson W. Oliver, Richard Caverly, Edward Fugier, John Sherry, George J. Campbell, William Robb, John F. O'Keefe, Robert Bruce, Isaac Shaw, Elmer Gormley, Richard Ryall, John J. Nolan, Orville Tobias, and Thomas McDonough; (middle row) John Hughes, John Healy, Patrick Hefferman, Frank R. Klotz, William Conboy, T. Brosnahan, John Mangold, James Earley, Fred Brown, Henry Mackenzie, Mike Conley, and Grant Allen; (back row) John Witt, P. M. Barrett, James McCue, Edward Kavanagh, S. J. Reardon, George Day, and William Taliaferro. Standing in the rear is A. J. Noble Jr.

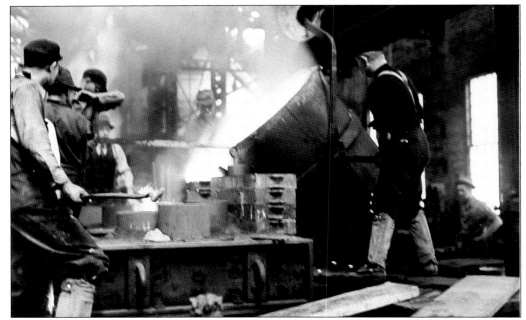

MARE ISLAND'S TRANSFORMATION. The 20th century ushered in the era of modern steel ships. Workers in the Mare Island foundry performed the dangerous job of pouring molten metal into molds to cast propellers and other parts. As Vallejo's foremost industry, Mare Island provided employment in a wide variety of trades including riggers, shipfitters, draughtsmen, painters, welders, machinists, mechanics, pipefitters, sailmakers, electricians, pattern makers, and scores of other skilled trades. (Official U. S. Navy photo.)

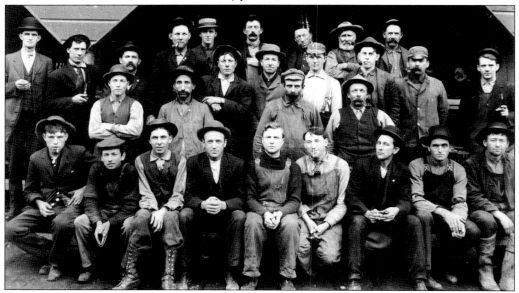

VALLEJO'S LUMBER INDUSTRY. Workers from the Aden Brothers Lumber Yard and Planing Mill pose for a group portrait. The Aden Brothers' facility was located at the foot of Santa Clara Street and sold coal, hay, and grain in addition to lumber. The Aden Brothers also operated a small shipyard and a ferry company.

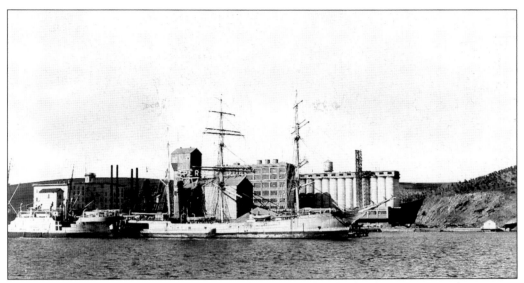

FLOUR MILL IN SOUTH VALLEJO. In 1860 John Frisbie chartered a ship to export wheat grown near Vallejo to Liverpool—the first shipment of wheat overseas from California. Captain A. D. Starr established Vallejo's first flour mill in South Vallejo in 1869. Flour shipped from the port of Vallejo would eventually travel to Asia, South America, and Europe as Vallejo became the largest flour shipping port in California. The mill was purchased by the Sperry Flour Company in 1910 and later became the General Mills Sperry Division.

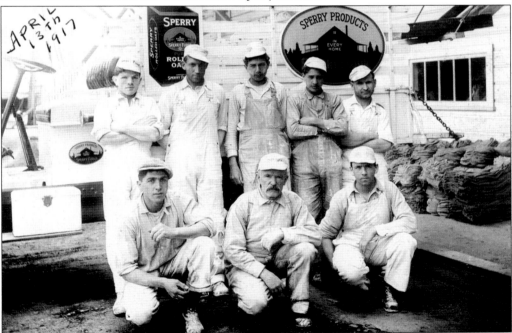

SPERRY MILLS EMPLOYEES. During World War I the Sperry Mills shipped tons of flour to Europe as part of the wartime relief effort. Employment at the mill increased from 125 workers in 1915 to 363 in 1919. Just after World War I, the mill hired a young, out-of-work actor who was employed briefly as a truck driver. His name was Boris Karloff.

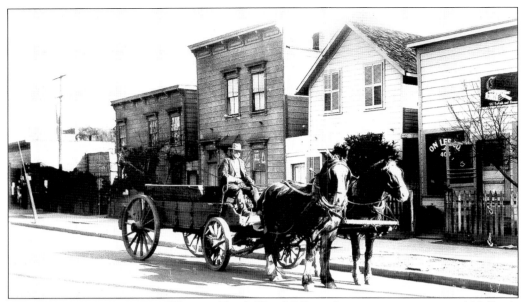

THE DOGCATCHER AND HIS WAGON. Frank "Deafy" Derrick was a veterinarian and Vallejo's pound master, or dogcatcher, for many decades during the early 20th century. Derrick was a colorful character—purportedly a former pony express rider, rodeo performer, wagon train scout, trick roper, silver miner, and an associate of Kit Carson and Buffalo Bill Cody. He was born near San Francisco's Mission Dolores in the 1840s and died in 1938.

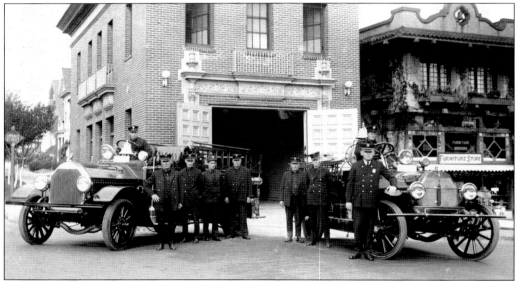

VALLEJO FIRE DEPARTMENT. Members of the Vallejo Fire Department pose in front of their station at the northwest corner of Sacramento and York Streets in this photo from the mid-1930s. Vallejo's earliest firefighters were members of volunteer hook and ladder companies. Early volunteer fire companies included the Vallejo Hook and Ladder Company, the San Pablo Engine Company, the Frisbie Engine Company, the Neptune Hose Company, and the Phoenix Engine Company. Firefighters were placed on the city payroll following the disastrous 1906 earthquake and fire in San Francisco.

PIONEER MARBLE AND GRANITE WORKS. Thomas and Robert Doyle were the proprietors of the Pioneer Marble and Granite Works, located at the northwest corner of Florida Street and Sonoma Boulevard. Examples of their skilled stone carving can be found in most of Vallejo's old cemeteries. Among their more important commissions was the imposing monument that marks the grave of General Mariano G. Vallejo in Sonoma.

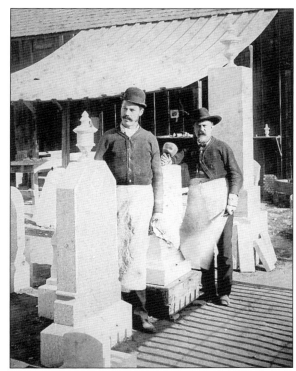

HEURTEUX'S SMOKE SHOP. Located at the corner of Georgia and Santa Clara Streets, Al Heurteux's Smoke Shop is shown here in an October 1906 photo. At the turn of the 20th century lower Georgia Street was the site of stores like Heurteux's, along with numerous restaurants and boarding houses. However, the first two blocks of Georgia Street also held 21 saloons.

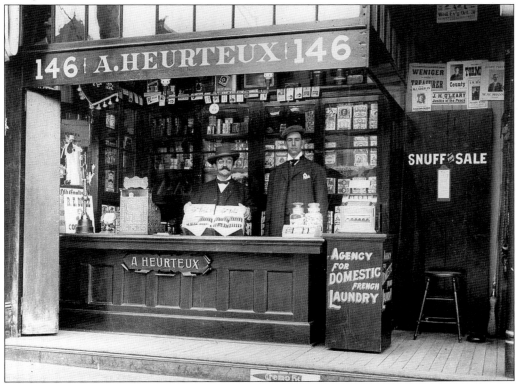

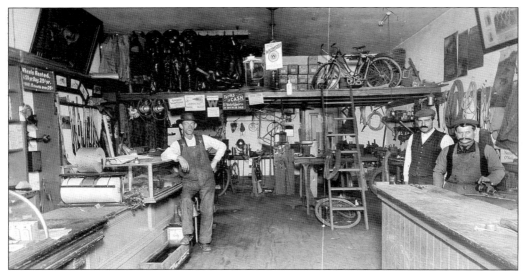

KING'S CYCLERY. William L. King capitalized on the popularity of bicycling at the turn of the 20th century. King (left) poses with other employees of King Cycling and Gun Store at 521 Marin Street. William King was the son of John L. King, first foreman of the Steam Engineering Department at Mare Island in the 1850s. William's uncle, Robert King, was Mare Island's first blacksmith.

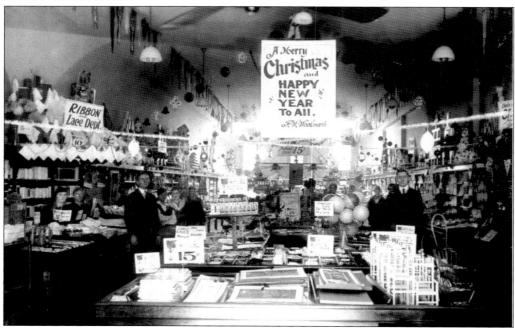

CHRISTMAS AT F. W. WOOLWORTH. In this December 1916 photo employees of F. W. Woolworth at 418 Georgia Street showed off their special holiday merchandise. Before the advent of suburban shopping malls, most of the major department stores were located in downtown Vallejo. Over the years, in addition to bargain stores like Woolworth's, Vallejoans could shop at major chains like Sears & Roebuck and J. C. Penney, or at high-end department stores like Levee's, Crowley's, and City of Paris.

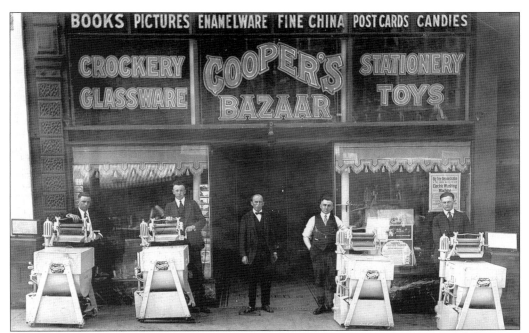

COOPER'S BAZAAR. In 1904 Johnston H. Cooper purchased a store called the Naval Bazaar at 217 Georgia Street. He soon changed the name to Cooper's Bazaar and a few years later moved to a new location at 229 Georgia Street. The store carried hardware, appliances, and other household goods. In this 1921 photo, Cooper (center) and several of his employees prepare to demonstrate four brand new, state-of-the-art electric washing machines.

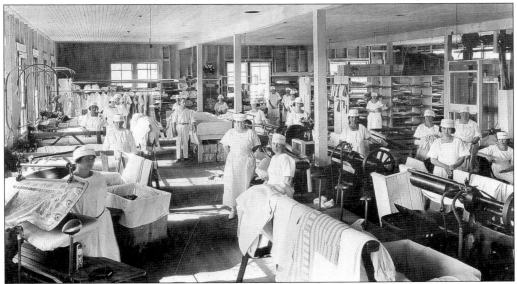

VALLEJO STEAM LAUNDRY. Workers at the Vallejo Steam Laundry take a break from their jobs to pose for a photograph. The laundry was established in 1893 at the southeast corner of Marin and Pennsylvania Streets. Although the work was often hard and tedious, one writer for the Vallejo *Times Herald* said that "to make wheels, gears, tubs, ironers, pressers, whirling dryers and quantities of soap and water all mesh together might better be called an art."

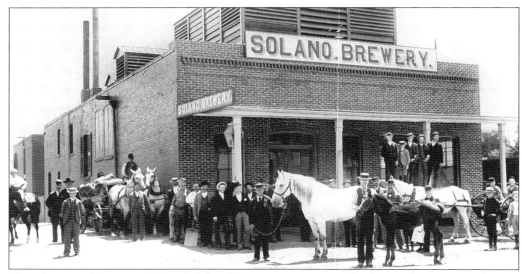

THE SOLANO BREWERY. Founded by German immigrants Charles Widenmann and Peter Rothenbusch, the Solano Brewery was renowned for its Solano Steam Beer. By 1891 the Marin Street facility had a brewing capacity of 6,000 barrels a year and boasted its own malting house. Charles Widenmann later bought out his partner and continued operating the brewery until 1918. Members of the Widenmann family were prominent in the area's political, educational, business, medical, and civic affairs for many years.

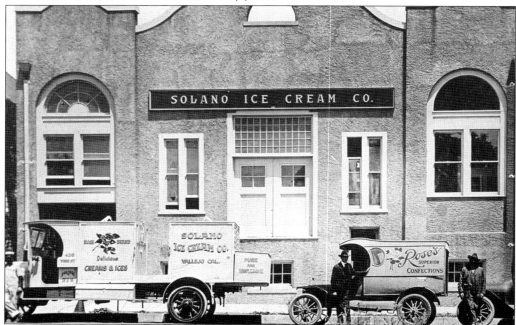

SOLANO ICE CREAM COMPANY. When Prohibition put the Solano Brewery out of business, the company's enterprising owners closed the Marin Street brewery and reinvented their business around the corner on York Street as the Solano Ice Cream Company. Nationwide prohibition took effect in 1919, but in Vallejo taverns and breweries within five miles of Mare Island were ordered closed in 1918 due to military restrictions imposed during World War I.

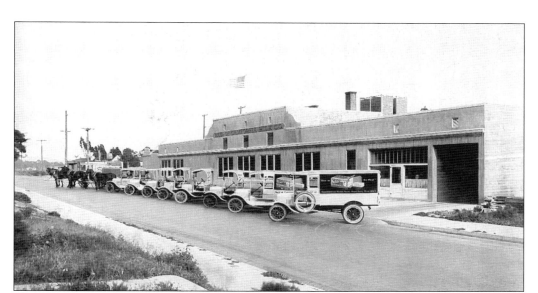

MAID OF CALIFORNIA. These delivery vehicles from Vallejo's Maid of California Milk Company illustrate the transition from horse-drawn wagons to motorized trucks in the 1920s. Brothers Dan, John, and Thomas Foley started the Foley Bros. Dairy in 1911, changing the name to Maid of California in 1922. Company president Dan Foley was appointed director of the California Dairy Council in 1923 and played a prominent role in Vallejo civic life for many years. Dan Foley Park was dedicated in his honor in April 1968.

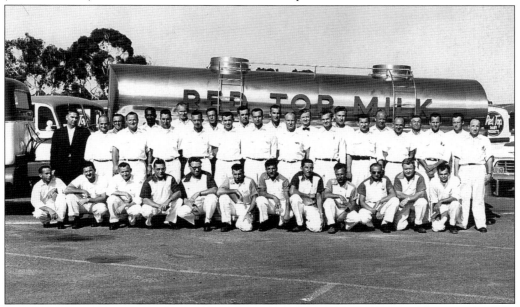

RED TOP DAIRY. For over a century the open hillsides surrounding Vallejo were prime land for raising dairy cows. One of the community's many dairies was Red Top Dairy, started in 1940 at the corner of Marin and Maine Streets. Other Vallejo dairies have included Lakeside Dairy, Union Creamery, Jersey Farm Creamery, and Maid of California Milk Company. Many prominent local families have been active in the dairy business in Vallejo, including the Mini, Foley, Borges, and Azevedo families.

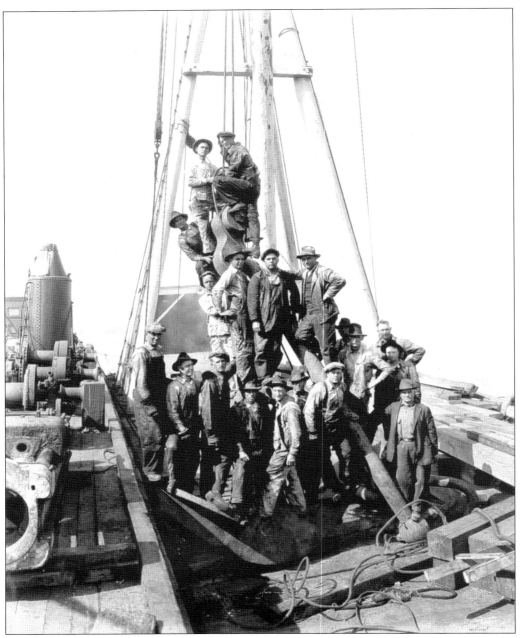

CONSTRUCTION OF THE CARQUINEZ BRIDGE. In 1924 these workers on the Carquinez Bridge were building the caissons used to support the bridge's massive center tower. The new bridge was described at the time as a "majestic masterpiece of engineering" and was heralded as the world's largest highway bridge. When it was finally completed in 1927, the total length of the new bridge was 4,482 feet and the main support towers stood 325 feet above the water. Fourteen thousand tons of steel were used in the project and five steel workers lost their lives during construction.

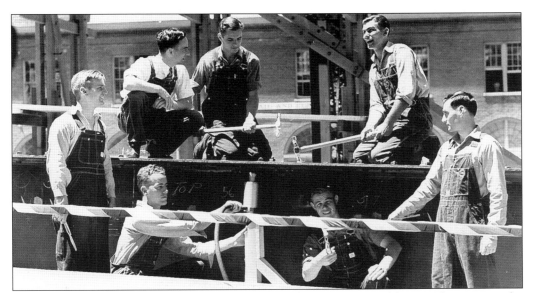

MARE ISLAND'S WORK FORCE EXPANDS. With the war clouds of World War II looming on the horizon, thousands of people from throughout the United States came to Mare Island for jobs in shipbuilding and repair. War had already broken out in Europe When these Mare Island workers celebrated the keel laying of the submarine tender *USS Fulton* on July 19, 1939. Pictured here, from left to right, are: (front row) Hugh Elsdon (standing), Bill Adams, Joe Burke, and Oliver Casagranda; (back row) Charles Dahme, Andrew Meyers, and John Wolff. (Official U. S. Navy photo.)

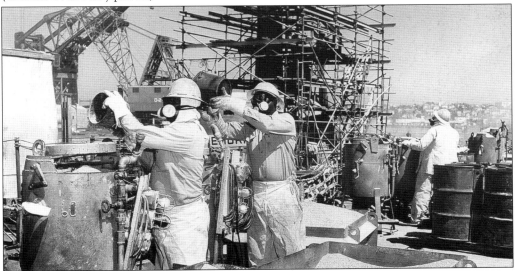

MARE ISLAND ENTERS A NEW ERA. Sandblasters from Mare Island's Shop 71 prepare to strip the hull of the submarine *USS Remora* in September 1956. After World War II the shipyard's workforce was reduced, but in the 1950s Mare Island was charged with a new mission: the construction, overhaul, and refueling of nuclear submarines. Traditional diesel-powered submarines like the *Remora* continued to arrive for overhaul, but the innovative nuclear-powered vessels offered a whole new set of challenges for Mare Island workers. (Official U. S. Navy photo.)

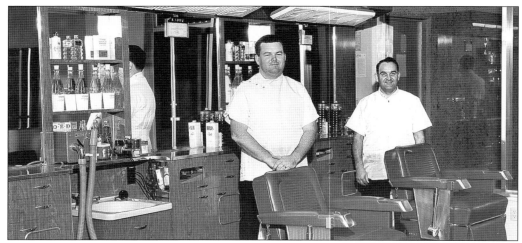

FLEMINGTOWN BARBERSHOP. Larry Dyke and Bill Fisher, proprietors of the Flemingtown Barbershop, celebrated their grand opening in October 1963. The barbershop and Renfrow's Restaurant were the first two businesses to open in the new Flemingtown Shopping Center, located at the corner of Tuolumne and Redwood Streets. As Vallejo expanded in the 1950s and '60s many new businesses opened in shopping centers like Flemingtown, Larwin Plaza, and the Springstowne Shopping Center. (Courtesy of Vallejo *Times-Herald*.)

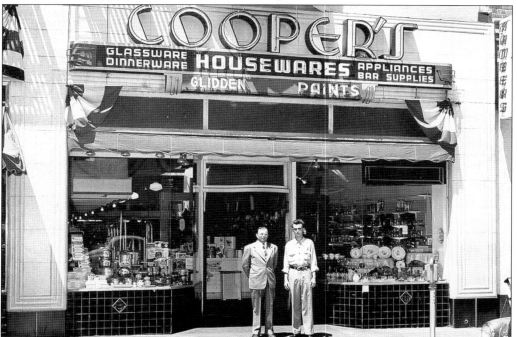

COOPER'S HOUSEWARES. In 1938 Johnston Cooper moved his store, Cooper's Bazaar, from 229 Georgia Street to 440 Georgia Street and changed the name to Cooper's Housewares. In 1949 the Cooper family opened a second location on Tennessee Street. Shown here are Cooper's son Kenneth (left) and grandson James in front of the Georgia Street store. Johnston Cooper served for many years on the Vallejo school board and was posthumously honored with the naming of Cooper Elementary School in 1954.

Three
VALLEJOANS AT PLAY

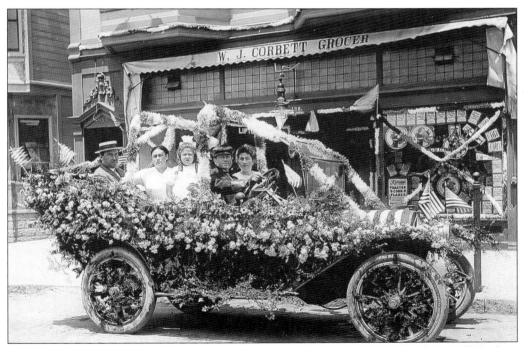

INDEPENDENCE DAY, 1912. Vallejoans really know how to have fun! In this photo, Bill Corbett and his family show off their beautifully decorated car, parked in front of their grocery store at 138 Virginia Street. The occasion was Vallejo's 1912 Fourth of July Parade. Corbett and William Scally shared the $20 prize for the two Best Decorated Automobiles in the parade. Vallejoans' leisure time activities have included community parades, street fairs, amateur athletics, musical groups, and community theater. For years residents have enjoyed abundant parks and playgrounds and have participated in a variety of diverse social and fraternal organizations.

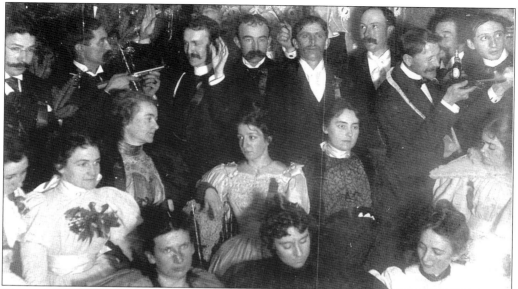

HAPPY HOLIDAYS, 1896. Miss Annie Pennycook hosted a holiday gathering of her close friends on Christmas Day, 1896. The celebration included refreshments, holiday games, and an exchange of gifts. Among those who enjoyed the festivities were, from left to right, A. E. Lucy, Lavina Bushnell, Ethel Cutler, Jean Brownlie, Estelle Lucy, Grace Brownlie, Maud Harrier, Maud Rounds, Belle Roney, A. L. Halliday, John Rothschild, Milton Cutler, G. G. Halliday, B. Beinenfeld, L. G. Harrier, Will Green, Johnston Cooper, James Topley, and Herbert Diamond. Pennycook was a teacher and principal in the Vallejo schools for more than 40 years, and Pennycook Elementary School was later named in her honor.

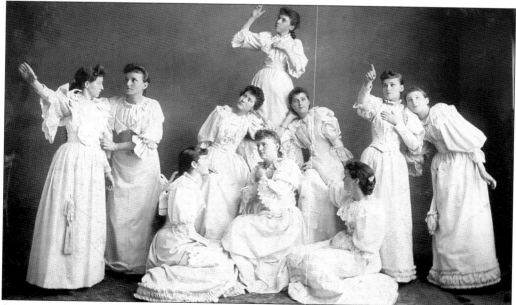

STRIKE THE POSE. The staging of historical and allegorical *tableaux* was a popular pastime during the 19th century. Each gesture had a special meaning. The young ladies posing here were members of Vallejo's Presbyterian Ladies Elocution Group.

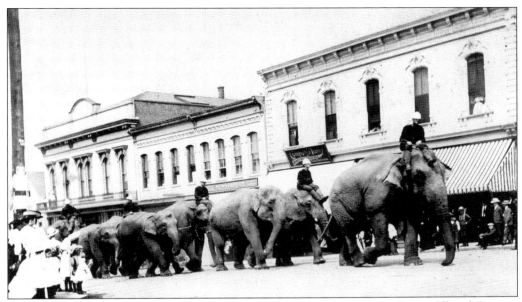

THE CIRCUS COMES TO TOWN! A herd of elephants parading down the middle of Georgia Street was a common sight around 1900 when the circus made its annual visit to Vallejo. Farragut Hall, a popular Georgia Street theater and concert hall, can be seen in the background (far left). Traveling circuses pitched their tents at the Cyclodrome racetrack at the end of Georgia Street, near present day Central Avenue.

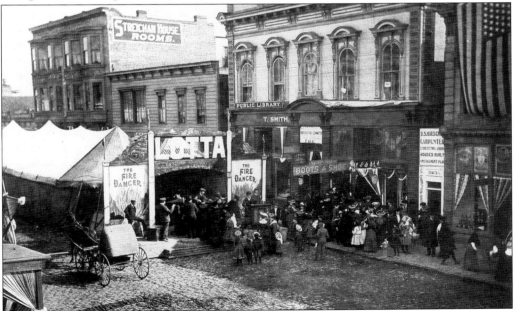

LOTTA THE FIRE DANCER. From its earliest days, downtown Vallejo has been the scene of parades, carnivals, festivals, and open-air markets. This c. 1900 downtown street fair was sponsored by the Fraternal Order of Eagles and featured the exotic Lotta the Fire Dancer. The Streichan House (background, at left) was built in 1899. The Times Building (at right) housed Vallejo's public library from 1891 to 1904.

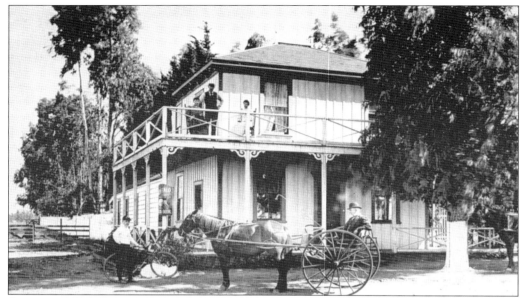

GERMANIA PARK. A popular Vallejo gathering spot was Germania Park, shown here in 1895. The park was located on Georgia Street, near present day Wallace and Solano Avenues. The adjacent Cyclodrome was a popular outdoor sports facility. Germania Park was operated by Larry Monreal until about 1915. Another popular local beer garden around the turn of the 20th century was Weniger's Gardens on Benicia Road.

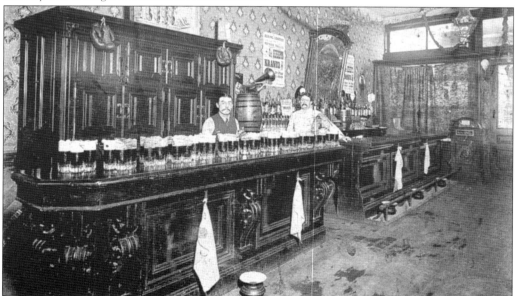

GETTING READY FOR THIRSTY CUSTOMERS. In this 1903 photo, Eugene Williams (right) was well prepared for thirsty patrons at his downtown Vallejo tavern. Georgia Street was a popular destination for boisterous sailors and Mare Island workers. Among the many saloons in downtown Vallejo at that time were the Waldorf, the Wave, the Enterprise, the Little Red Rock, the California, the Klondyke, the Davy Crockett, the Leader, the Philadelphia House, and the Richelieu.

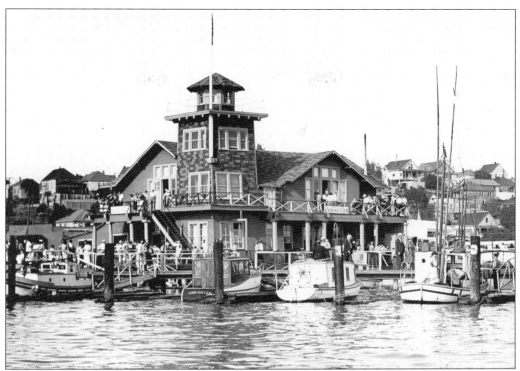

VALLEJO YACHT CLUB. The Vallejo Yachting and Rowing Club was established in 1900. Its first commodore was William J. Wood, a master sail maker at Mare Island. The club obtained a site at the foot of Virginia Street, and architect Carl Siebrand, who had previously designed Seattle's yacht club, drew up plans for their new building. The yacht club was constructed with volunteer labor, and its long history in the community reflects Vallejo's significant maritime heritage.

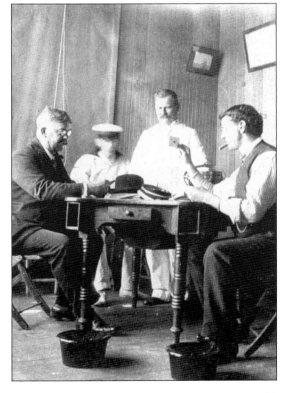

JACK LONDON AT THE VALLEJO YACHT CLUB. A frequent visitor to Vallejo was author Jack London, shown here playing cards at the yacht club around 1913. Pictured here, from left to right, are George F. Hilton, unidentified, Judge John Browne, and London. The *Roamer*, London's yacht, was often berthed at the club, and London himself spent much time around Vallejo and Benicia as a young man. His adventures up and down the Carquinez Straits were detailed in his book, *Tales of the Fish Patrol*.

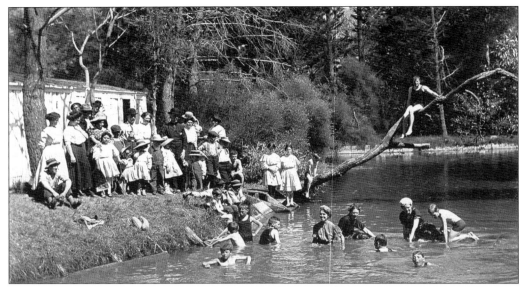

SWIMMING AT BLUE ROCK SPRINGS. By the early 1870s Blue Rock Springs, then known as White Sulphur Springs, had become a popular resort. People from throughout northern California visited the resort for the medicinal qualities of the spring water. Around the turn of the 20th century local families used the park for summer camping, swimming, picnics, and hiking. For many years the resort was operated by the Madrid family. The City of Vallejo purchased the property in 1937.

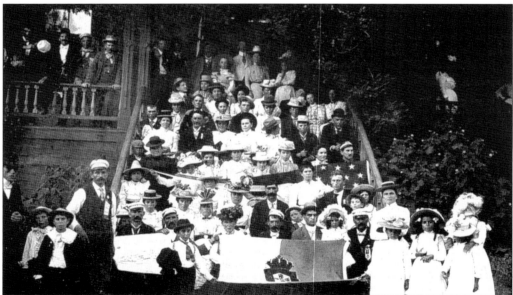

PORTUGUESE PICNIC AT BLUE ROCK SPRINGS. Members of Vallejo's Portuguese community gathered for a portrait on the steps of the Blue Rock Springs hotel around 1900. Portuguese immigration to Vallejo dates well back into the 19th century when many Portuguese fishermen settled in South Vallejo. Later, Portuguese families became active in dairy ranching in the area. Among the many Portuguese social organizations active in Vallejo is the *Sociedade Da Coroa Do Divino Espirito Santo*.

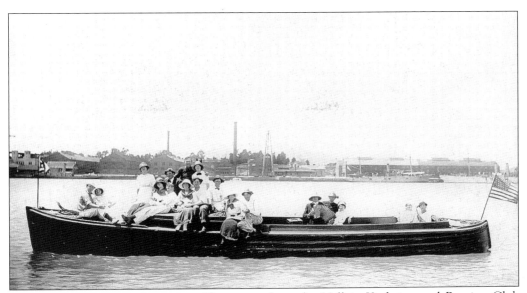

BOAT RACES ON THE CHANNEL. This group from the Vallejo Yachting and Rowing Club enjoyed a Memorial Day outing in 1912. Boat races between local teams date back to at least 1867, when several navy teams competed on the Mare Island Channel. Five years later a Fourth of July regatta pitted Vallejo's Farragut Boat Club against two boat clubs from San Francisco. By 1879 Vallejo's Alert Boat Club had a four-oar wood shell, a four-oar paper shell, a racing barge, and two Rob Roy canoes at their boathouse on the Georgia Street wharf.

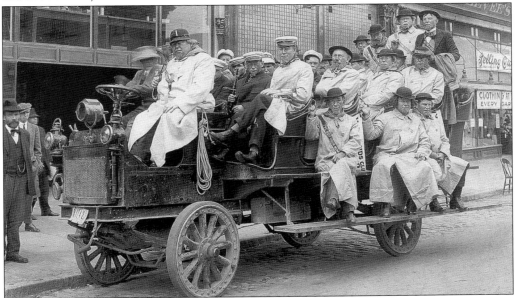

WIELAND CLUB OUTING. Members of Vallejo's Wieland Club depart for a picnic at Boyes Hot Springs in Sonoma County in June 1913. The Vallejo *Evening Chronicle* reported that only 25 club members could fit into their 34-passenger bus " . . . owing to the fact that the Wielands run in large sizes, some of the members being as big as two or three ordinary sized men." A second vehicle was quickly pressed into service. The newspaper also complimented "the Dutch comedy make-up worn by the members."

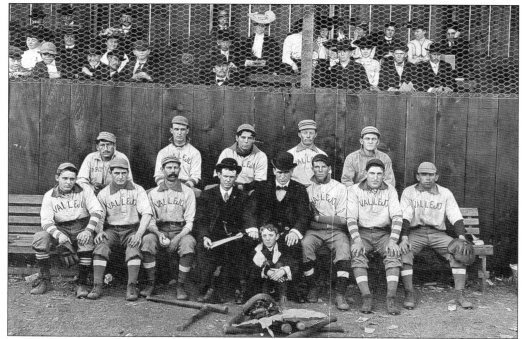

VALLEJO BASEBALL CHAMPIONS OF 1903. Led by their ace pitcher, Jack Ward, Vallejo's semi-professional baseball team battled to win the championship of the Central California League in 1903. The team played its games at the Cyclodrome on Georgia Street. In 1919 Vallejo built a new ballpark, called Beach Park, at the foot of Virginia Street. Beach Park was named for Mare Island's popular commanding officer, Captain Edward Beach.

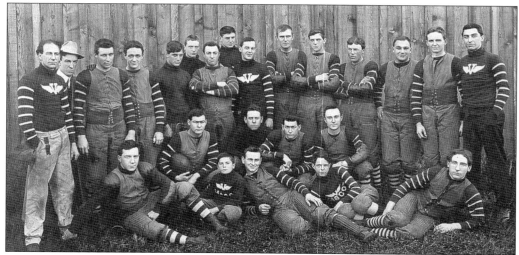

THE WINGED VS. Although they only played from 1905 to 1911, the Winged Vs amateur football team rolled up an astounding winning record and became the undisputed football champions of northern California. Over a span of six years the team had 65 wins, with only one loss and three ties. Many team members went on to prominent careers, including Columbus Castagnetto (Solano County auditor), Oscar Hilton (elected to the California State Assembly), Jack Thornton (Solano County sheriff) and Harry Gee (Vallejo city attorney).

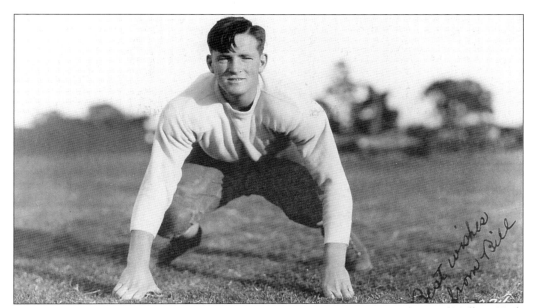

A Vallejo Sports Legend. Football great Bill Corbus was a 1929 graduate of Vallejo High School. Corbus was a two time All-American guard at Stanford (1932 and 1933) and a charter member of the Stanford Football Hall of Fame. He was inducted into the National College Football Hall of Fame in 1957. Corbus Field at Vallejo High School was named in his honor.

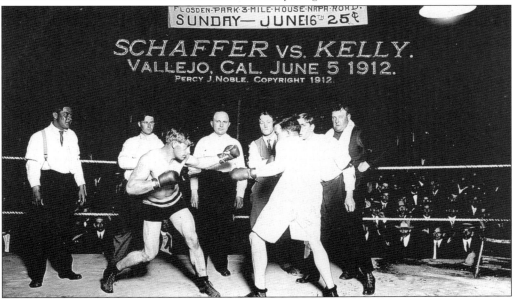

Boxing Match at the Flosden Arena. Jack Kelly and Vallejoan Bill Schaffer were among the boxers battling it out at the Flosden Arena on June 5, 1912. According to the Vallejo *Evening Chronicle*, "those who went out to the big Flosden arena got every cent of their money's worth . . . . Kelly gave the heavyweight [Schaffer] little chance for infighting. . . and for a couple of rounds he had the sailor going some. Schaffer's strength stood him in good stead, however, and the bout proved to be a good one." The Flosden Arena was near the present day intersection of Broadway and Highway 37.

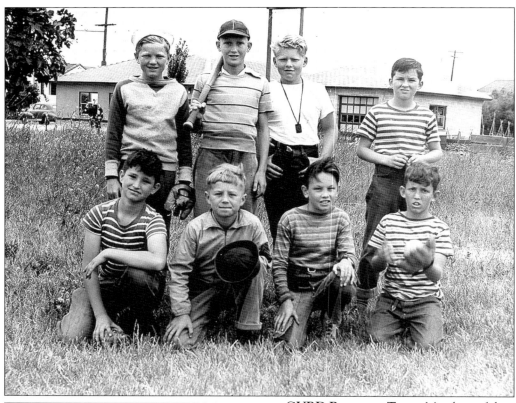

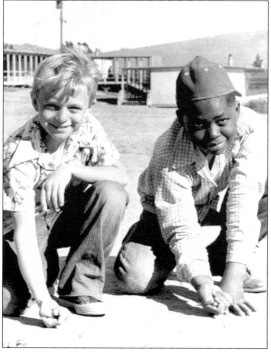

GVRD Baseball Team. Members of the "Little Apaches" baseball team prepare to meet their opponents at Curry Playground in this 1944 photo. The Greater Vallejo Recreation District grew out of the Vallejo Recreation Commission, which was organized in 1937. In addition to managing Vallejo's many parks and community centers, GVRD also sponsored youth sports teams, playground activities, crafts, a day camp program, and public pools.

GVRD Marble Tournament. Dale Yost (left) and Bill Mitchell, who were described by the Vallejo *Times-Herald* as "a couple of Chabot Terrace sharpshooters," are shown here practicing for the Greater Vallejo Recreation District's 1949 Marble Tournament. The tournament was held at Washington Playground on April 24, and Nathaniel Kilgore, a sixth grade student at McKinley School, won the championship over 350 other contestants after a series of morning and afternoon elimination rounds.

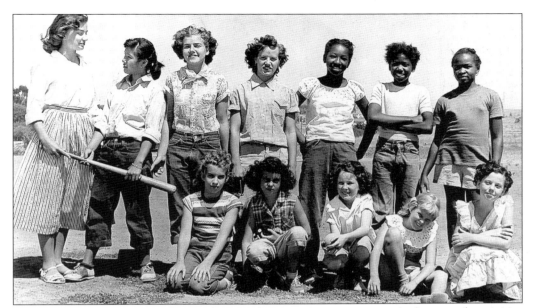

GVRD Girls' Softball Team. Among the many team sports and playground activities sponsored by the Greater Vallejo Recreation District was girls' softball. This 1951 team, from left to right, included: (first row) Barbara Gee, Janice Kephart, Sue Byram, Marilyn Ward, and Clara Jean McPhillips; (back row) "Rusty" Torykian, Pat Orpilla, Dorothy Buchanan, Barbara Buchanan, Algene Ross, Barbara Claibourne, and Annie Sampson.

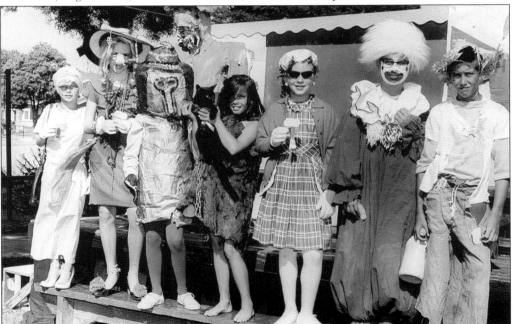

GVRD Tacky Day Fair, 1963. The Tacky Day Fair was held each year at Washington Playground from 1939 to 1972 under the sponsorship of the Greater Vallejo Recreation District. Prizes were awarded for the best costumes and best activity booths. Vallejo kids had their own planning committee for the event, selecting the annual theme and working out other details.

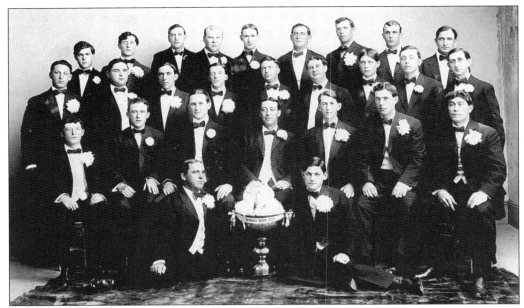

SNOWBALL SOCIAL CLUB. The members of the Snowball Social Club pose for a group photo during their annual Initiation Banquet on June 6, 1909. The banquet, according to the Vallejo *Evening Chronicle*, was "more fun... than has been witnessed at any of the social organizations in Vallejo for some time." The Snowball Social Club was a popular organization for young people and held regular dinners, dances, and outings.

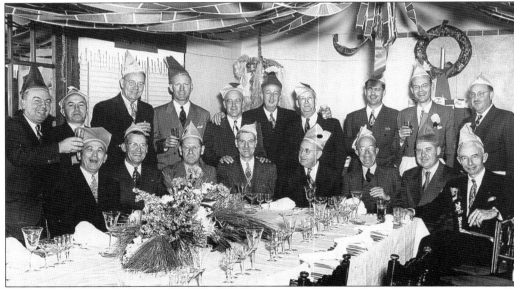

ALL WORK AND NO PLAY. In April 1887 a group of Vallejo businessmen formed the Vallejo Township Board of Trade, predecessor to the Vallejo Chamber of Commerce. The chamber helped promote Vallejo businesses, but not all of its activities were strictly work related. Chamber members also took time out to enjoy social occasions with their colleagues in the Vallejo business community. In this 1947 photo, chamber members enjoy their annual Christmas party.

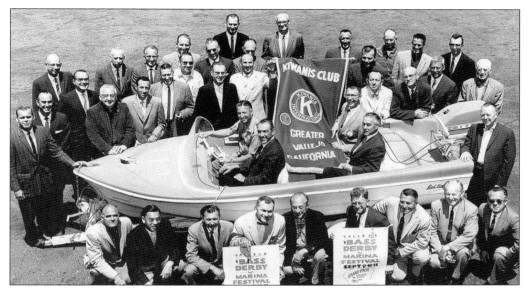

VALLEJO KIWANIS BASS DERBY. Members of the Greater Vallejo Kiwanis Club are shown here with the motorboat and trailer that they awarded as top prize in their 1960 Bass Derby. Kiwanis is one of the many service clubs and fraternal organizations that have been active in the community throughout its history. Others include Vallejo Rotary, Soroptimist International, Knights of Columbus, Native Sons of the Golden West, the Masonic Temple, Vallejo Elks, Vallejo Moose Lodge, Redmen's Lodge, Lion's Club, and Oddfellows. (Courtesy of Vallejo *Times-Herald.*)

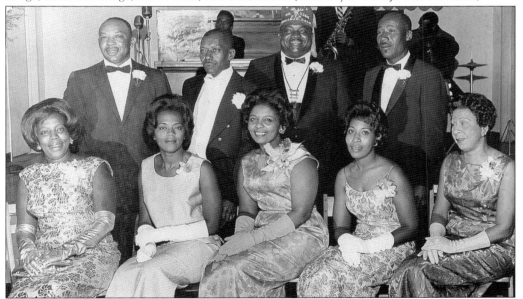

NAVY CITY ELKS. In December 1964, the Navy City Elks Lodge celebrated its 15th anniversary with a dinner for more than 300 people, including dignitaries from Elks lodges from throughout the bay area. Members of the planning committee for the event pictured here, from left to right, are: (front row) Leona Sutton, Jessie Williams, Gloria Scales, Earline Wroten, and Mary Stephens; (back row) James Garner, Howard Monroe, Earl Batiste, and Olivet Ezell. (Courtesy of Vallejo *Times-Herald.*)

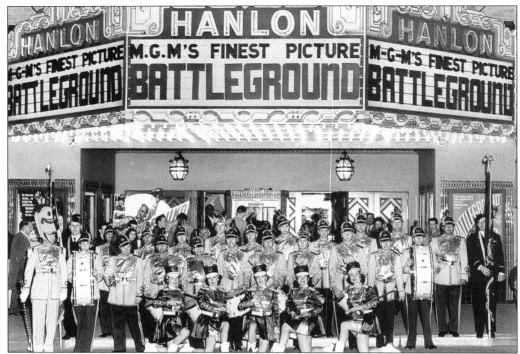

HANLON THEATER, 1949. The Hanlon Theater at 414 Virginia Street was built in 1920 and was one of Vallejo's most popular movie theaters for nearly 35 years. Vallejo movie palaces opened and closed and underwent frequent name changes over the years. In addition to the Hanlon, other movie houses in Vallejo included the Marval, the Fox Senator, the Victory, the Rita, the Empress, the El Rey, the Valmar, and the Strand.

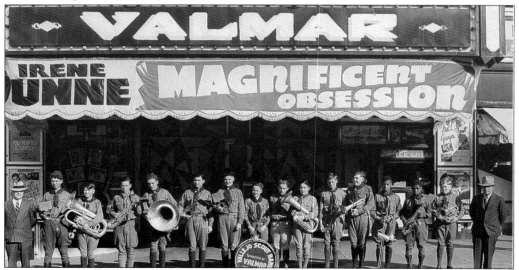

VALMAR THEATER, 1935. The Vallejo Boy Scout Band was sponsored by the Valmar Theater, which was located at 206 Georgia Street. Shown here with the band are Valmar co-owners P. S. MacDonald (far left) and Louis Trager (far right). In 1937 the Valmar was purchased by the Fox West Coast Theaters chain.

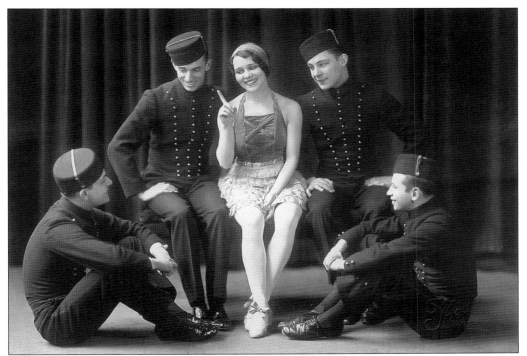

LODENA EDGCUMBE. For nearly forty years Lodena Edgcumbe was an active supporter of the arts and culture in Vallejo. As a professional dancer she performed around the world, but her greatest commitment to dance was as a local teacher. For years she taught dance to hundreds of Vallejo's children and nurtured their interest in the performing arts. Edgcumbe arrived in Vallejo as an infant—an orphan of the 1906 San Francisco earthquake. She was adopted by a local family when attempts to find her birth family proved unsuccessful.

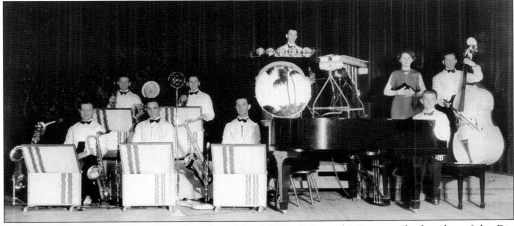

VALLEJO'S BIG BAND ERA. The decades of the 1920s, '30s, and '40s were the heyday of the Big Bands. Most of the big name national bands played in Vallejo at the Casa de Vallejo, Veterans Memorial Hall, and the Dream Bowl. Vallejo's own local bands were also popular favorites at dances and concerts. The Ken Harris Orchestra is shown here playing at the Veterans Memorial Hall in 1935. Other popular local bandleaders included Roy Graff, Jimmy Emerson, Hal Hay, Keith Kimball, Gene Gelling, and Lou Boss.

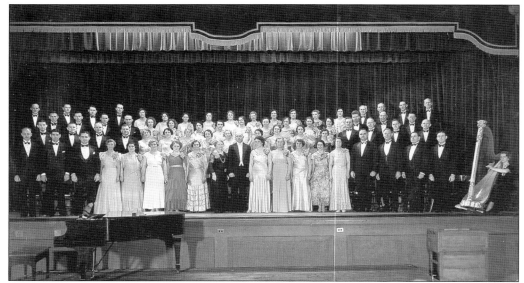

VALLEJO CHORAL SOCIETY, 1933. Stormy weather failed to deter a crowd of nearly 1,000 people on the evening of December 12, 1933. The Vallejo Choral Society, under the direction of Kenneth R. Dick, performed a concert of Christmas favorites accompanied by pianist Clara B. Thomas. A harpist from San Francisco, Miss Eleanor Costello, also performed in the program, held at the Veterans Memorial Auditorium.

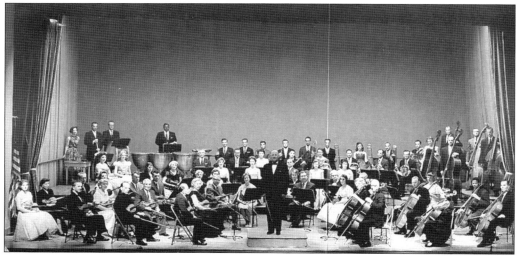

VALLEJO SYMPHONY ORCHESTRA. Established in 1931, the Vallejo Symphony is one of the oldest symphony orchestras in northern California. The symphony held its debut performance at the Veterans Memorial Auditorium under the direction of conductor Julius Weyand. Since that time the orchestra has played an important role in the cultural life of the community. The orchestra moved to the Hogan Junior High School Auditorium in 1954. This photograph shows the symphony with conductor Virl Swan in 1958.

CELEBRATING THE ARTS. A variety of Vallejo arts and cultural organizations held a Fine Arts Fiesta at the Solano County Fairgrounds on October 24, 1965. Shown here preparing for the event are, from left to right, ticket chairman Louis Sanders, Vallejo Artists League member Marilyn Unruh, and Vallejo Symphony Association president David Max. The list of participating groups shown in the photo represents just a few of the many diverse cultural groups in the community. (Courtesy of Vallejo *Times-Herald*.)

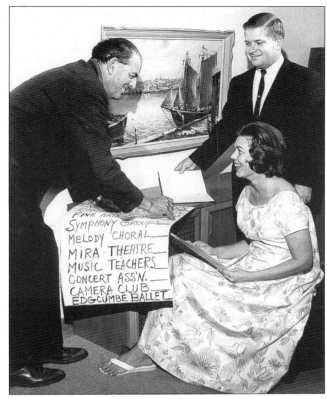

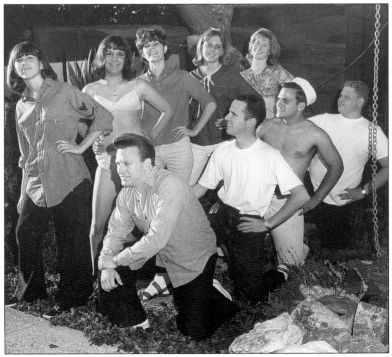

SONGS FROM SOUTH PACIFIC. Members of the Vallejo Choral Society performed selections from *South Pacific* at a concert at the Hogan High School Auditorium on June 4, 1966. Pictured here, from left to right, are: (front row) Stan Reich, Bob Kurtz, Carl Cornils, and Bob Mattheis; (back row) Donna Crow, Pat Freeman, Debby Guntrum, Anne Hopper, and Barbara Brandt. (Courtesy of Vallejo *Times-Herald*.)

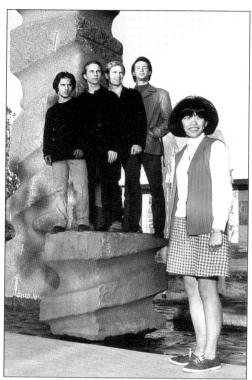

CHINESE TEEN CLUB DANCE. Betty Cheung, queen of the Vallejo Chinese community, poses with the Four-Way Stop Band in this March 1969 photo. The band was scheduled to play for a Chinese Teen Club dance at the Vallejo Community Center on Amador Street. Band members, from left to right, included Steve Woodbury, Roy Rogers, Winston Wallace, and Alan Bogner. Rogers would later go on to enjoy a long career as a popular blues musician and record producer. (Courtesy of Vallejo *Times-Herald*.)

OPENING OF THE MIRA THEATER. State Senator Luther Gibson cuts the ribbon to open the new MIRA Theater on February 22, 1968. The theater opened in the former Bay Terrace Elementary School on Daniels Avenue. The MIRA Theater Guild grew out of the Mare Island Recreation Association that had been established during World War II. On Gibson's right is Vallejo Mayor Florence Douglas. To his left is MIRA Theater Guild representative Dollie Nunn.

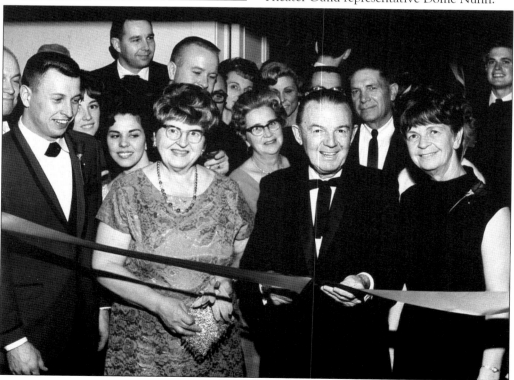

Four
VALLEJO GROWS UP
1901–1940

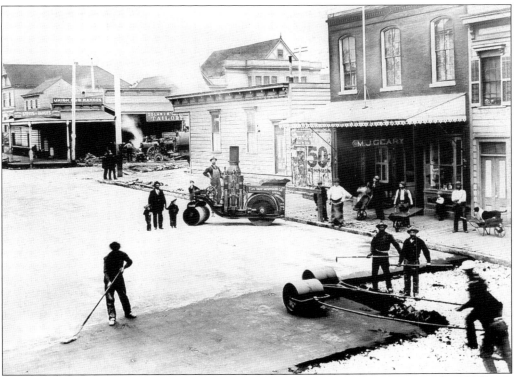

PAVING VALLEJO'S STREETS. Primitive dirt roads became a thing of the past when Vallejo's downtown streets were paved, but the wooden plank sidewalks remained. This photo, taken around 1912, shows a street paving crew hard at work at the intersection of Georgia and Santa Clara Streets. As Vallejo entered the 20th century the community grew from a quiet village into a thriving city. Major civic improvements included a new library, post office, city hall, and several new churches. Vallejo gained full advantage from the 20th century's amazing new innovations in communication, transportation, and technology.

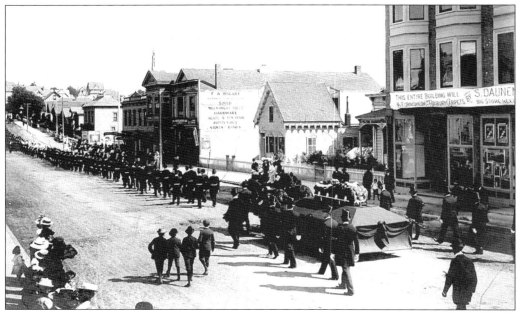

VALLEJO MOURNS THE DEATH OF PRESIDENT MCKINLEY. Vallejoans began the new century by gathering in mourning after the assassination of President William McKinley. On Thursday, September 19, 1901, hundreds of Vallejoans formed a public procession that wound through the streets of downtown. The procession was led by members of the Vallejo Police Department, and also included a cavalry detail from the Benicia Barracks, a U. S. Marine Corps unit from Mare Island, a group of Vallejo Civil War veterans, and representatives from various local fraternal organizations.

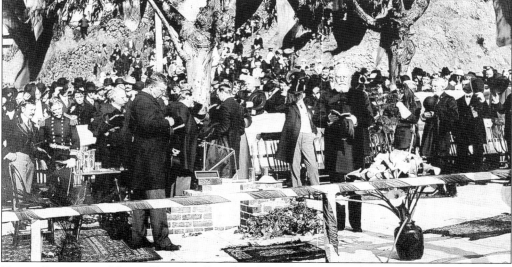

TEDDY ROOSEVELT VISITS VALLEJO. President Theodore Roosevelt visited Vallejo on May 14, 1903 to lay the cornerstone for the new Naval YMCA on Santa Clara Street. Roosevelt was the second U.S. president to visit Vallejo. The first was Rutherford B. Hayes in 1880. President Roosevelt is shown here bowing his head as Chaplain Adam McAlister delivers the invocation at the cornerstone ceremony.

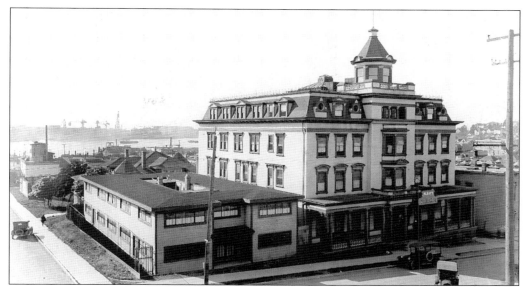

THE NAVAL YMCA. This Vallejo landmark was built through the hard work and financial support of Mrs. Bowman McCalla, wife of Mare Island's commandant. It opened in 1904 and was the second oldest YMCA in the United States and the first to be established on the West Coast. The building was designed by architect W. J. Cuthbertson and built at a cost of $62,000. At one time, the Naval YMCA boasted the only elevator in Solano County. The building was demolished in 1958.

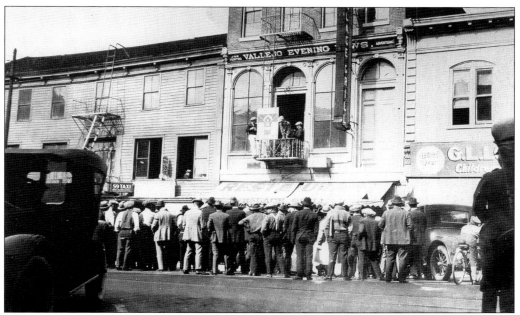

A BASEBALL "BROADCAST." In the days before radio was widespread, people still clamored for up-to-the-minute news of their favorite baseball teams. In this photo, Vallejoans gather around the Vallejo *Evening News* office to follow the game. Newspaper employees would receive the play-by-play via telegraph or radio and describe the game to the crowd gathered below, illustrating the position of each runner on a large board.

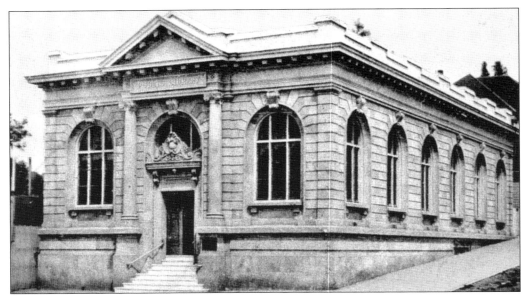

VALLEJO'S CARNEGIE LIBRARY. Industrialist Andrew Carnegie donated money to communities across the United States to build public libraries. In 1903 Carnegie offered $20,000 to the City of Vallejo to erect a new library, with the provision that in return the city provide at least $2,000 each year for its operation. Vallejo's Carnegie Library was located on the northwest corner of Virginia and Sacramento Streets. It was dedicated on July 4, 1904.

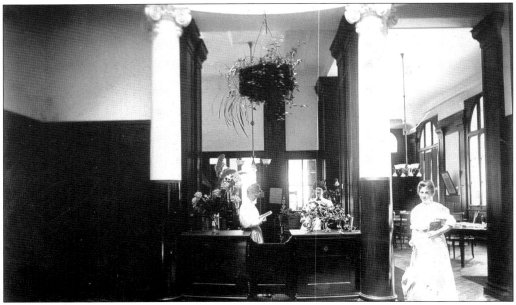

CARNEGIE LIBRARY ROTUNDA. The lobby of Vallejo's Carnegie Library was topped by an elegant dome. Miss Gertrude Doyle (center, standing behind plant) was appointed librarian in 1898, when the library was still located in the Times Building on Georgia Street. Doyle served as librarian for 46 years. Upon her retirement in 1944, Agnes Walsh was appointed head librarian. Vallejo's Carnegie Library, a beautiful historic landmark, was torn down in 1970 as part of the downtown redevelopment project.

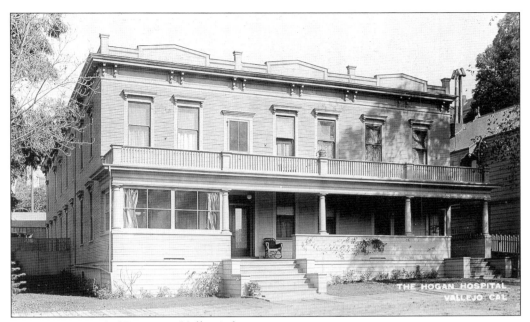

DOCTOR HOGAN'S HOSPITAL. Vallejo's first hospital was founded by Dr. James J. Hogan around 1907. It was located at the northeast corner of Virginia Street and Sonoma Boulevard. The facility was later purchased by Thomas "Tobe" Williams. The hospital proved inadequate to handle the demands of the 1918-19 influenza epidemic, so a new hospital was built on Tennessee Street in 1921. The building pictured here was later moved to Morrow Cove for use by the Rodeo-Vallejo Ferry Company.

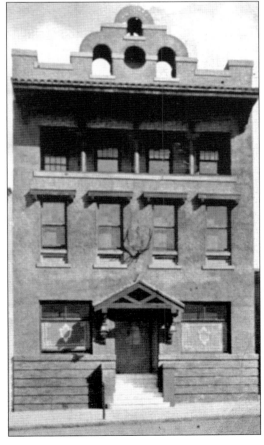

VALLEJO ELKS HALL. The Vallejo Elks Lodge was first organized in 1900. After meeting in several temporary locations, the lodge purchased the old Hibernian Hall on the east side of Sacramento Street between Georgia and Virginia Streets. The Elks met at this location for eleven years until they moved into the former John Frisbie mansion at the corner of Virginia and Sutter Streets. After the Elks departed this hall on Sacramento Street, it became home to the Salvation Army.

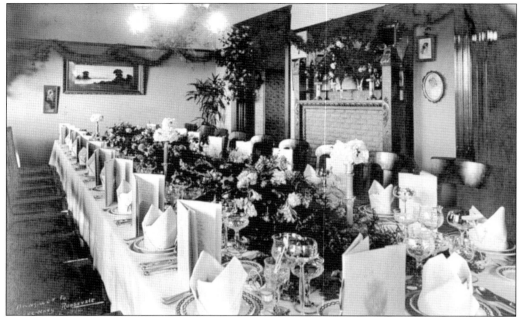

FDR Visits Vallejo. In April 1914 Assistant Secretary of the Navy Franklin Roosevelt visited Vallejo to assess Mare Island's suitability to build a new battleship. On Friday, April 16, Roosevelt and his wife, Eleanor, were feted at a banquet at the Vallejo home of Judge Frank Devlin. "The banquet accorded me last night," Roosevelt commented, "was something I will never forget." Mare Island eventually was awarded the contract to build the battleship *USS California*.

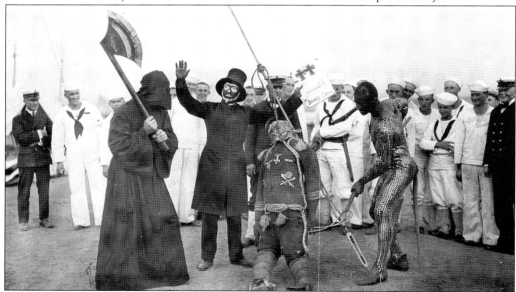

Vallejo During World War I. Anti-German sentiment ran high across the United States during the first World War, and Vallejo was no exception. In this photo, *c.* 1918, characters representing the Grim Reaper, an undertaker, and the Devil hang Germany's Kaiser Wilhelm in effigy as amused Mare Island sailors look on. Many young men from Solano County answered the call to serve during World War I, and 48 of them lost their lives in the conflict.

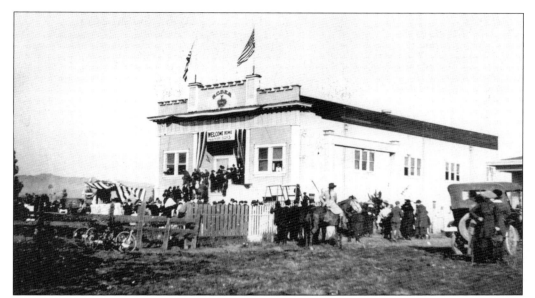

WELCOMING HOME THE BOYS. At the end of World War I, members of Vallejo's Portuguese community decorated their meeting hall with flags, banners, and a sign that said "Welcome Home to Our Boys." The SCDES Hall on Contra Costa Street was built in 1915 and has been the site of numerous festivals, dinners, and other social activities.

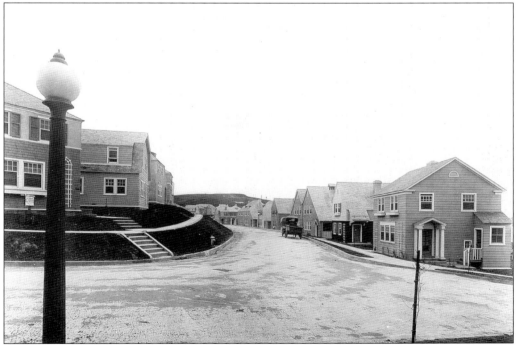

BAY TERRACE. During World War I, wartime expansion at Mare Island brought about the need for additional U.S. Navy housing in Vallejo. In 1918 the new Georgetown housing project was dedicated. The U.S. Post Office soon pressed for a name change, since California already had a Georgetown in Placer County. Vallejo's "Georgetown" then became known as Bay Terrace.

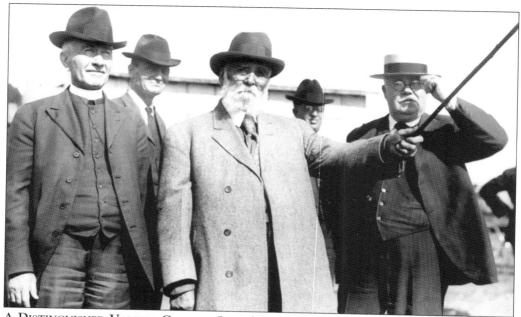

A DISTINGUISHED VALLEJO CITIZEN. One of the honored guests at the 1923 groundbreaking ceremony for the new Carquinez Bridge was Dr. Platon Vallejo (center). Dr. Vallejo was a son of General Mariano G. Vallejo and was the first native-born Californian to become a licensed physician. His long and eventful life spanned major events in California and U. S. history. Among his earliest memories was the Bear Flag Rebellion of 1846. He later served in the Civil War and during his lifetime saw the invention of the automobile, airplane, electric light, telephone, and numerous other modern conveniences. Dr. Vallejo died in 1925.

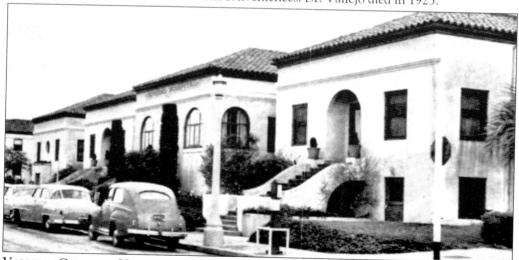

VALLEJO GENERAL HOSPITAL. Tobe Williams was the manager of the Vallejo General Hospital, built in 1921 at the corner of Tennessee and Sutter Streets. Although thousands of Vallejoans received health care there, perhaps the hospital's most notorious "patient" was gangster Baby Face Nelson, who used the hospital as a hideout in 1934. Williams later served time in prison for his role in harboring Nelson. Despite his underworld connections, Williams is still remembered for his many positive contributions to the community.

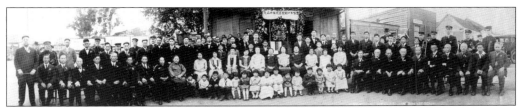

CHINESE COMMUNITY MEMORIAL SERVICE. In April 1925, Vallejo's Chinese community gathered to mourn the death of Dr. Sun Yat-sen, father of Chinese nationalism. In 1904 Sun Yat-sen spent several months in the bay area, promoting the Chinese nationalist movement. Throughout its history, Vallejo's Chinese community has had many active social, political, and community welfare organizations. The Hop Sing Tong was established in Vallejo in the late 19th century. At the turn of the 20th century, the Chinese Nationalist League and the Young China Association were both active. Beginning in the 1930s, the Nu Chi Club sponsored numerous social events.

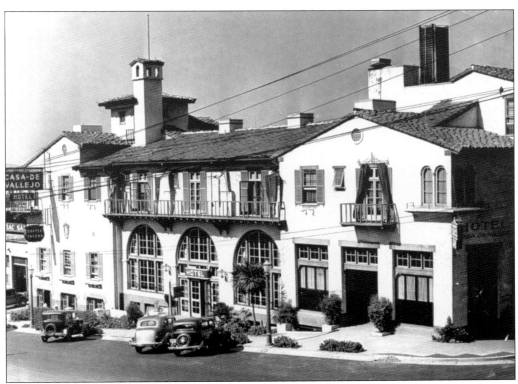

CASA DE VALLEJO. Built in 1919 as the Industrial YMCA, the Casa de Vallejo was acquired by Harry Handlery in the 1920s, redecorated with a Spanish theme, and reopened as a luxury hotel in 1928. Throughout the 1930s and '40s the Casa de Vallejo hosted many of the top entertainers of the Big Band era. A major expansion took place on the eve of World War II, and the hotel remained a thriving center for community events through the 1950s and '60s.

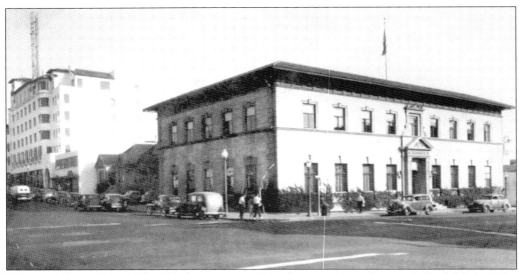

VALLEJO CITY HALL. The 1920s was a period of prosperity and growth for Vallejo. The opening of the Carquinez Bridge in 1927 put Vallejo on the main highway connecting San Francisco with Sacramento and points east. That same year Vallejo opened a new city hall at 734 Marin Street. The Spanish Renaissance Revival building was designed by architect Charles Perry. In 1975 a new city hall was built on Santa Clara Street and the old city hall became the home of the Vallejo Naval and Historical Museum.

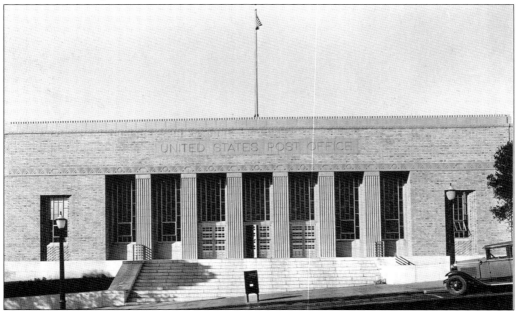

VALLEJO POST OFFICE. During the Great Depression the federal government sponsored public works projects to create jobs. One such federally funded project was the Vallejo Post Office, located on the west side of Marin Street, between Capitol and Carolina Streets. The cornerstone of the building was laid on April 15, 1933. The post office lobby features a large tile mural created by the Gladding, McBean Company depicting the dedication of Mare Island's first floating drydock.

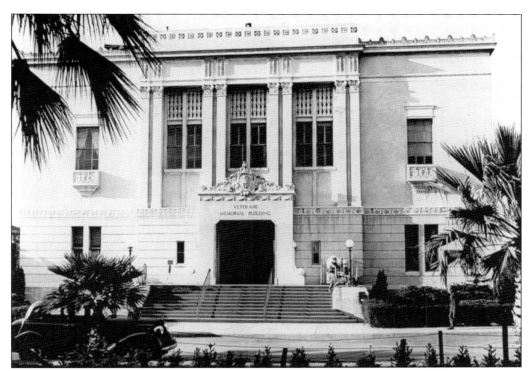

HONORING VALLEJO'S VETERANS. The Veterans Memorial Building at the corner of Marin and Alabama Streets was dedicated in 1930. The popular meeting hall was designed by the Sacramento architectural firm of Coffman, Sahlberg, and Stafford. The hall has been the site of meetings for various veterans organizations and community groups, as well as concerts by local and nationally-know musical acts.

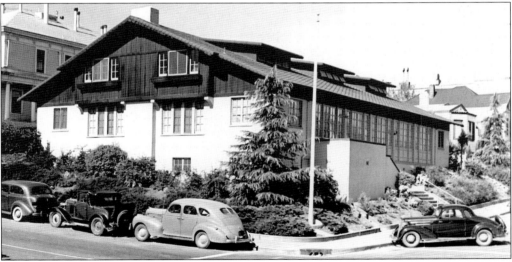

VALLEJO WOMEN'S CLUB. Built in 1921 as Vallejo's YWCA and designed by renowned California architect Julia Morgan, this building became the Vallejo Women's Club in 1927. The Arts and Crafts style architectural gem was located at the corner of Sacramento and York Streets. Unfortunately, it was demolished in the early 1960s.

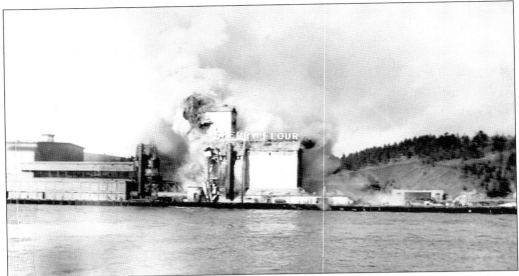

SPERRY MILLS FIRE. On August 30, 1934, a spectacular fire destroyed a large portion of the Sperry Flour Mill. Two marine elevators, 21 bins of grain, and 500,000 grain bags were consumed by the flames. Vallejo Fire Department crews were aided by floating fire equipment from Mare Island. Explosions of grain dust blew huge sheets of corrugated metal off the roof of the mill and 6,000 tons of grain was destroyed before the blaze was finally brought under control.

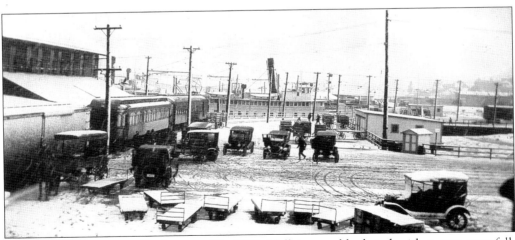

A RARE SNOWSTORM. On January 29, 1922, Vallejo was blanketed with a rare snowfall. Although only three inches fell on the city, its weight was enough to topple telegraph poles. Local children (and some adults) built snowmen, and the buses between Vallejo and Benicia were unable to complete their runs. Vallejo also had significant snowfalls in 1887 and 1913.

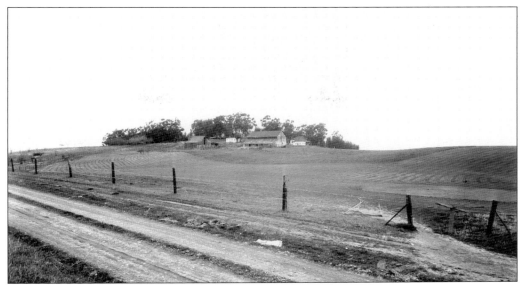

MORTGAGE HILL. In 1930 Tuolumne Street was still just a dirt country lane. The barns and outbuildings on the hill in the background were located on the grounds of the former Good Templar's Orphans Home. By 1930 the area had become the Vallejo Municipal Golf Course. At the end of that decade the hill would be developed into the Vista de Vallejo subdivision, also known as "Mortgage Hill." This section of Tuolumne Street is near the present day intersection with Valle Vista Avenue.

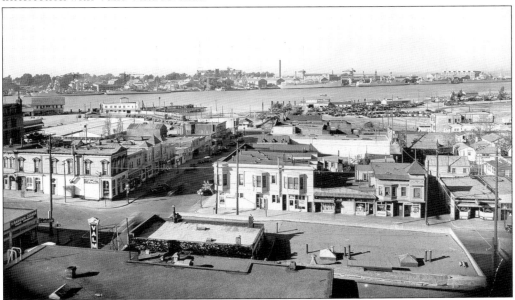

VALLEJO'S WATERFRONT IN THE 1930s. Vallejo had a thriving waterfront in the early decades of the 20th century. This view shows the intersection of Georgia and Santa Clara Streets, looking west. By the mid-1930s the city's population was about 30,000. Although the Great Depression put thousands out of work nationwide, Vallejo fared much better due to the steady flow of work at the Mare Island Navy Yard. In the 1930s Vallejo referred to itself as "the City of Cash" because of the large federal payroll at Mare Island.

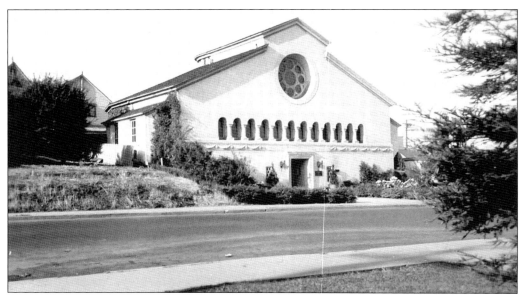

FIRST CHURCH OF CHRIST, SCIENTIST. Built in 1929, the First Church of Christ, Scientist at 733 Kentucky Street was noted for its unique architecture and beautiful stained glass windows. The Christian Science denomination first met in Vallejo in 1904, but it took nearly 25 years before they were able to build their own church. The church was designed by architect Henry Gutterson.

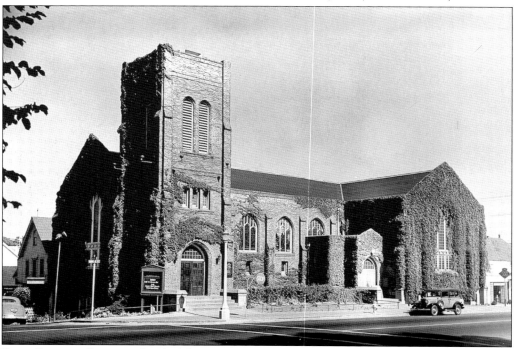

FIRST BAPTIST CHURCH. In 1916, having outgrown their church building on Capitol Street, the congregation of the Cornell Baptist Church purchased a lot at the corner of Sonoma Boulevard and Carolina Street. The congregation reincorporated as First Baptist Church and broke ground for their new church in 1922. The church building was dedicated on May 17, 1925.

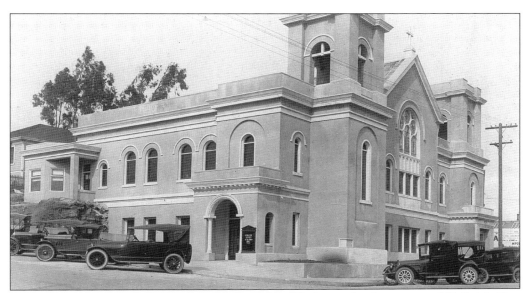

FIRST PRESBYTERIAN CHURCH. Rev. Nathaniel B. Klink was the first pastor of Vallejo's First Presbyterian Church, founded in 1862. In the following year construction began on a new church building at the corner of Marin and Carolina Streets on land donated to the congregation by General John Frisbie. After nearly 60 years, the original church building proved inadequate, so a new church building, pictured here, was built in 1920.

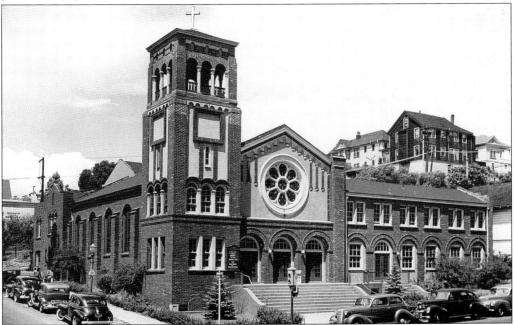

FIRST METHODIST CHURCH. The northeast corner of Virginia Street and Sonoma Boulevard was the site of Vallejo's first hospital. In 1919 the First Methodist Church purchased the property and began construction of a new church. Prior to that time their church had been located a half block farther west on Virginia Street. The newly completed church was dedicated on April 22, 1923.

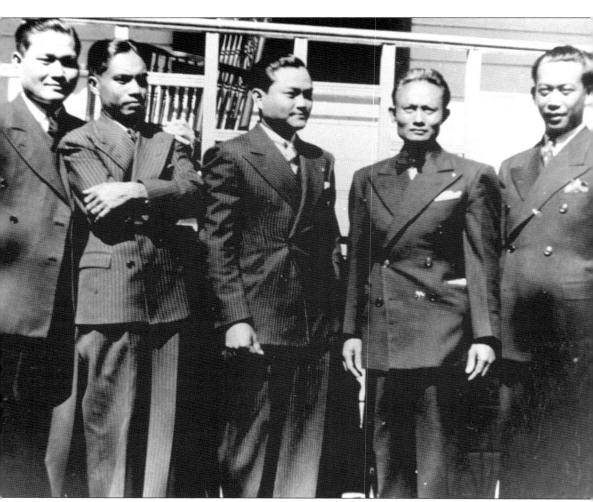

VALLEJO MANONGS. A group of young Filipino men poses for a photo *c*. 1940. From left to right are Basilio Madayag, unidentified, Pete Saltiban, unidentified, and Nazario Orpilla. Vallejo's Filipino community dates back well over a hundred years. In 1898 the U.S. Pacific Fleet defeated the Spanish Navy at the Battle of Manila Bay during the Spanish-American War. The United States acquired the Philippines at the end of that conflict and young Filipino men began to serve as stewards aboard U.S. Naval vessels. Many of those vessels returned to Mare Island, marking the beginning of Vallejo's Filipino community. The young men of that first generation of Filipino immigrants, known as manongs, lived in a thriving community of boarding houses in downtown Vallejo. Immigration restrictions prevented these men from bringing wives or families to the United States. Fraternal organizations like the *Legionarios del Trabajo* and *Caballeros Dimas Alang* fostered a sense of community among these newly arrived Filipino immigrants.

Five

GETTING AROUND TOWN

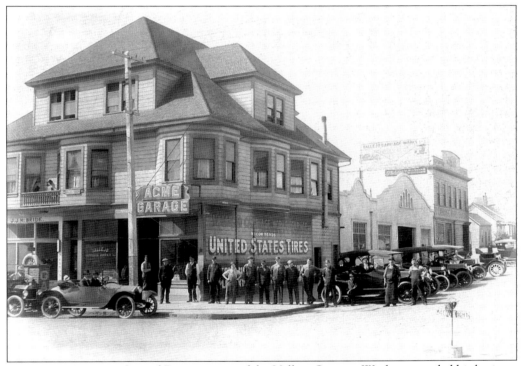

THE ACME GARAGE. Conrad Rump, owner of the Vallejo Carriage Works, expanded his business to include the Acme Garage and thereby successfully made the transition from the horse and buggy era to the modern age of the automobile. The Acme Garage was located at the southwest corner of Marin and Capitol Streets. Transportation has played a key role in the development of the City of Vallejo. Ferries connected Vallejo with the rest of the bay area. Railroads arrived in the 1860s and provided passenger and freight service between Vallejo and other California communities. In the 1920s the Carquinez Bridge offered a major highway link and spurred phenomenal growth. From the very beginning, Vallejoans have traveled by land, by sea, and by air.

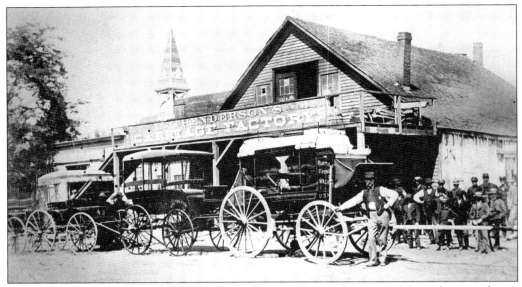

HENDERSON CARRIAGE FACTORY O. L. Henderson's carriage factory on Marin Street is shown in this photograph from the 1870s. The newly made carriages on the street in front of the building were delivered to the town of Williams in the Sacramento Valley, where they served passengers traveling from Williams to the famous Bartlett Springs resort in Lake County. Henderson was a Civil War veteran who later served as Solano County sheriff.

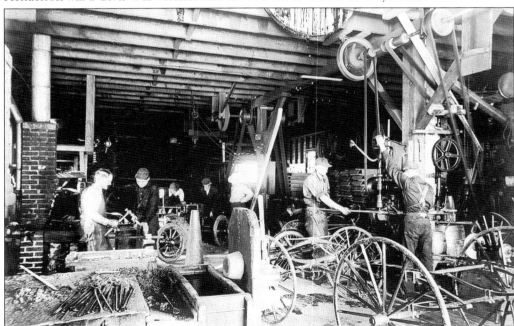

STARR CARRIAGE WORKS. Frank H. and William J. Ripson owned and operated the Starr Carriage Works at 132 Virginia Street. Their carriage works built and repaired all types of horse-drawn vehicles and they employed blacksmiths, wheelwrights, and woodworkers. Other Vallejo carriage makers in the horse-drawn days included Conrad Rump's Vallejo Carriage Works on Capitol Street and O. L. Henderson's carriage factory on Marin Street.

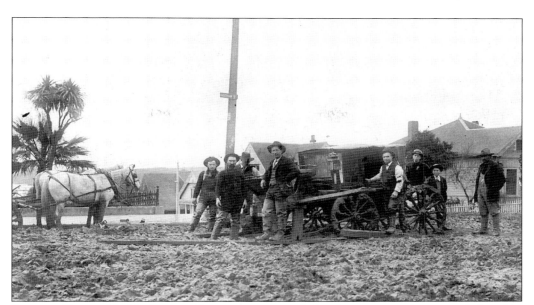

BOGGED DOWN. Muddy Georgia Street was no match for this group as they struggled to free their hack from the mire. The photo was taken around 1905 and the hack (a horse-drawn cab) belonged to Alexander Gill's Capitol Street Stables. Paving of Vallejo's downtown streets began around 1911. By August 1912, 87 Vallejo streets had been paved.

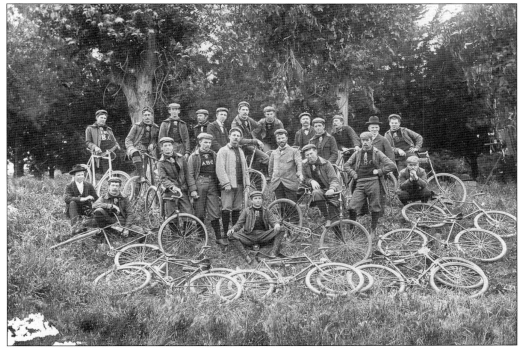

GETTING AROUND BY BIKE. Hard working members of the Ariels, Vallejo's chapter of the American Bicycle Club, built a 14-mile cinder path from Vallejo to Napa with wooden bridges over the small streams. Some of the club's members in this 1902 photo include, from left to right, Sam Cooper, James J. Hogan, Grant Luper, Charles Miller, Ralph Finnell, and E. B. Hussey.

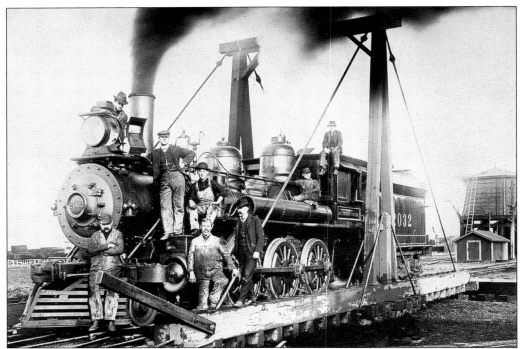

RAILROAD TERMINUS. The California Pacific Railroad established its southern terminus at South Vallejo in 1867. Trains that ran from Calistoga, Sacramento, and Santa Rosa were turned around on a turntable at the foot of Lemon Street once they arrived in Vallejo. The California Pacific was eventually taken over by the Central Pacific Railroad. Locomotive No. 2032 is shown here on the turntable around 1901.

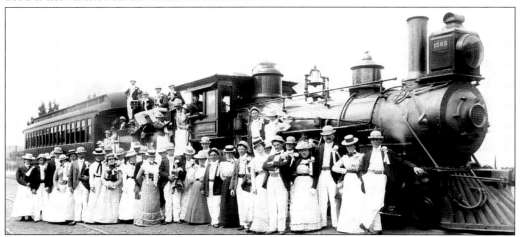

EXCURSIONS BY RAILROAD. Members of Vallejo's Snowball Social Club made frequent trips by rail to neighboring communities or on outings in the Sonoma County countryside. The railroad provided Vallejo with a valuable link to the rest of California for both passengers and freight. At one point the California Pacific Railroad operated 16 locomotives out of its southern terminus at Vallejo. The early locomotives were named for the railroad's founders or for cities along the route. Among them were the *Wm. Mason*, the *J. M. Rider*, the *D. W. Rice*, the *D. C. Haskin*, the *Yolo*, the *Elmira*, and the *Solano*.

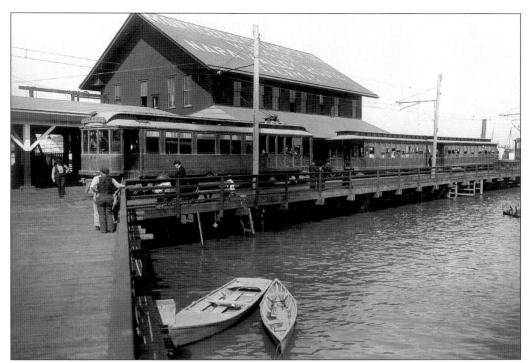

THE MONTICELLO WHARF. In 1906, passengers disembarking from ferries at the foot of Georgia Street could catch an electric train at the Monticello wharf and ride as far north as Yountville. By 1912 the route was extended to Calistoga and the electric trains eventually made as many as ten round trips a day between Vallejo and cities to the north. From the wharf, the tracks ran up the center of Georgia Street, turned left on Sonoma Boulevard, and continued north to Napa. Electric interurban train service ended in 1937.

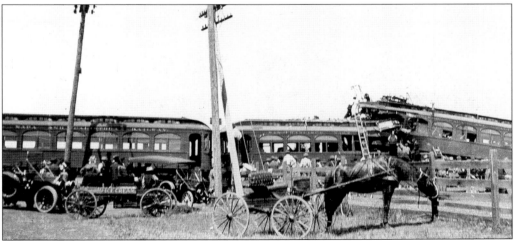

TRAIN WRECK OF 1913. On June 19, 1913, a northbound interurban train collided head-on with a southbound train coming from Napa. The tragic wreck, about two miles north of Vallejo, claimed 13 lives and injured nearly 60 others. An eyewitness to the collision, Miss Minnie Hauhuth, carried seriously injured passengers to the Vallejo hospital in her car and then transported nurses back to the crash site to provide first aid.

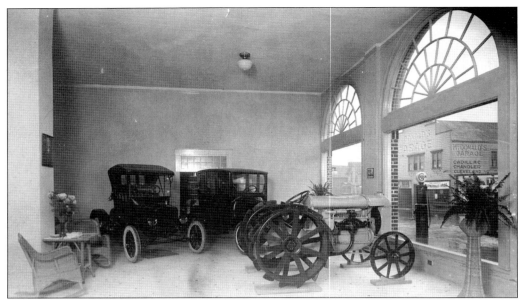

ACME GARAGE, C. 1925. In the 1920s Vallejoan's could buy a new Model T Ford (or a tractor) from the Acme Garage at 227 Capitol Street. Vallejo auto dealers in the early years of the 20th century sold many makes and models of cars. Most of the manufacturers of those early cars have long since gone out of business, but brands like Stutz, Packard, Jeffrey, Kissell, Maxwell, and Overland are memorialized in the names given to Vallejo's downtown alleys.

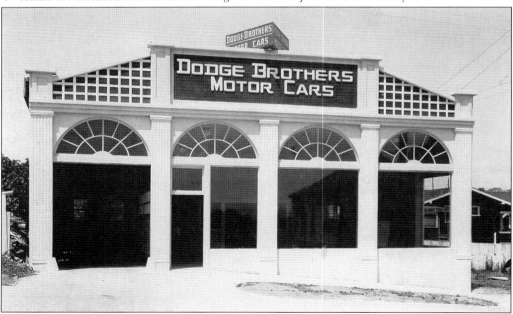

DODGE BROTHERS MOTOR CAR DEALERSHIP. One of Vallejo's early automobile dealerships was this one operated by George Dalwigk on Sonoma Boulevard. Dalwigk moved his Dodge franchise to Virginia Street by the late 1920s. Other Vallejo auto dealers in the 1920s included Herman Freudenberg, L. M. Dudley, Vallejo Motor Sales, Rump & Kennedy, and the Kern Motor Company.

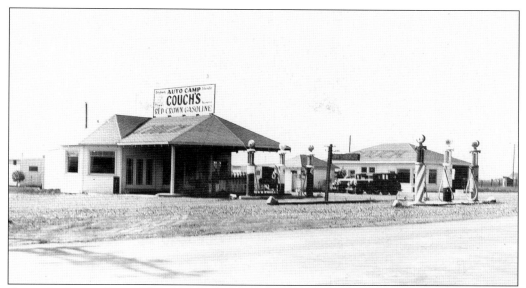

COUCH'S AUTO CAMP. Throughout the 1930s and '40s Couch's Auto Camp served as a way station for travelers arriving in Vallejo. The busy naval shipyard at Mare Island attracted workers from throughout the United States. Many of those arriving in Vallejo seeking new opportunities stayed at Couch's until they could find permanent accommodations. Couch's was located at the intersection of Sonoma Street Extension and Napa Road, today the intersection of Broadway and Couch Street.

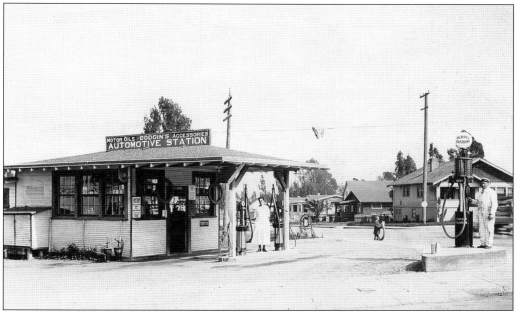

FILL 'ER UP! One of Vallejo's early service stations was Dodgin's Automotive Station, located at the corner of Kentucky Street and Napa Road (now Broadway). Ads for the station in the 1920s boasted "Dodge In: The Most Modern Service Station in Northern California." After the Carquinez Bridge opened in 1927 Napa Road became the route of the cross-country Lincoln Highway through Vallejo.

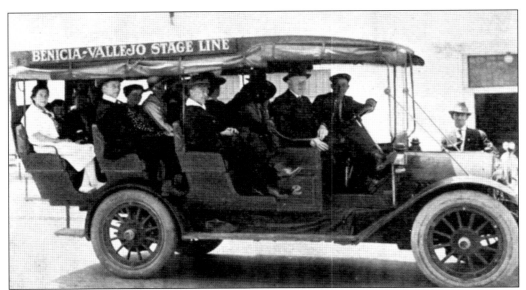

BENICIA-VALLEJO STAGE LINE. Milo Passalacqua started the Benicia-Vallejo Stage Line in 1915. He is shown here driving one of the company's two 1914 Buicks. Passalacqua's bus service made connections between Benicia, Mare Island, and the ferry wharves and electric train stations in Vallejo. When Milo was drafted to serve in World War I, his brother Joe took over operation of the company.

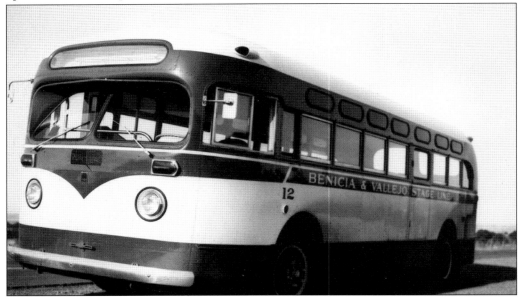

A NEW BUS FOR THE BENICIA-VALLEJO STAGE LINE. The Benicia-Vallejo Stage Line continued operations through the mid-1960s, but it was not the only bus company to serve Vallejo. Hartley Lowell started the Vallejo Bus Company around 1919. In 1935 the company was acquired by Victor Raahauge of the Mare Island Ferry Company. Ownership changed again in 1940, and by 1944 the City of Vallejo was running the company. During World War II, the U.S. Navy operated a fleet of 300 buses to handle the many defense workers coming to Vallejo from surrounding communities.

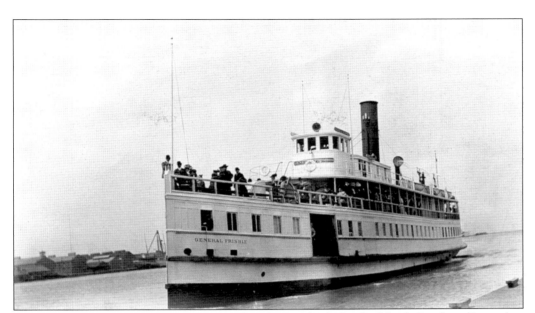

THE GENERAL FRISBIE. The ferry *General Frisbie* was built for the Hatch Brothers Steamship Company and began service in Vallejo on June 2, 1901. The *General Frisbie* made three daily round trips from Vallejo to San Francisco. On December 14, 1918 the *General Frisbie* rammed the ferry *Seahome* in dense fog on San Pablo Bay. Since both vessels were moving very slowly, no passengers were injured. The *General Frisbie* survived the crash but the *Seahome* sank soon after the accident.

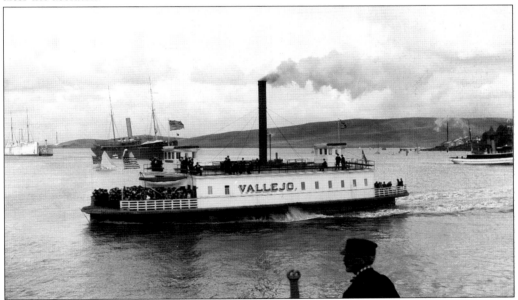

THE FERRYBOAT VALLEJO. Built in 1879, the side-wheel ferry *Vallejo* carried workers back and forth between Vallejo and Mare Island for nearly 70 years. After she was retired from service the *Vallejo* became a houseboat in Sausalito. Among the houseboat's well know residents were Zen philosopher Alan Watts and artists Gordon Onslow Ford and Jean Varda. In 2004 the historic ferry was still afloat in Sausalito.

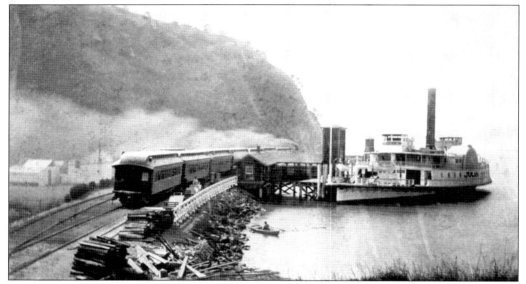

THE FERRYBOAT JULIA. The side-wheeler ferry *Julia* was built in 1864 and operated for many years on the Sacramento and San Joaquin Rivers. She was later acquired by the Central Pacific Railroad and made regular trips between South Vallejo and Vallejo Junction on the Contra Costa side of the Carquinez Straits. The *Julia* is shown here loading passengers at Vallejo Junction.

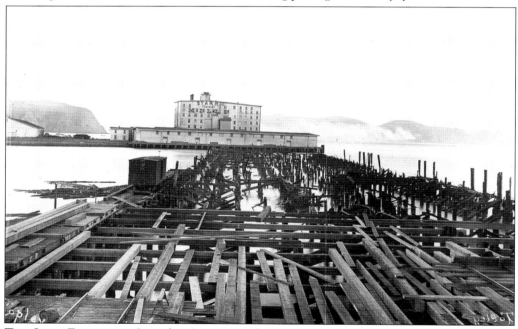

THE JULIA EXPLOSION. Just after 6 a.m. on February 27, 1888, the ferryboat *Julia* sounded her whistle to announce her departure from the South Vallejo dock. Moments later, the *Julia* was ripped apart by a tremendous boiler explosion that destroyed the ferry and set fire to the wharf. Thirty people were killed in the blast and many others were injured. This photograph shows the charred wreckage of the wharf. In the background is the Starr Flour Mill, built in 1869 and demolished in 1958.

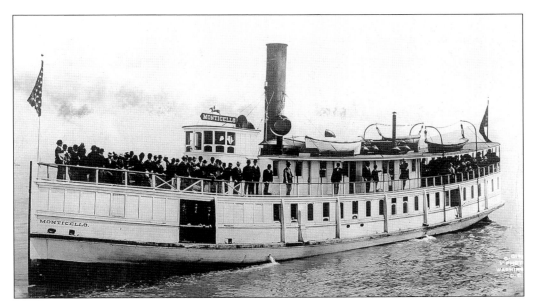

MONTICELLO STEAMSHIP COMPANY. The ferry *Monticello*, built in Ballard, Washington, was the first ferry operated by the Hatch Brothers Steamship Company in Vallejo. The Hatch brothers acquired several other ferries and later changed the name of their company to the Monticello Steamship Company. Following the 1906 San Francisco earthquake and fire the *Monticello* delivered emergency supplies to the city and ferried refugees back to Vallejo.

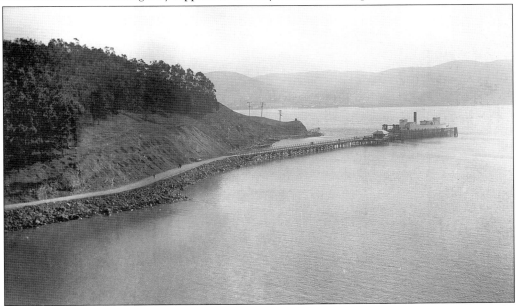

THE SIX MINUTE FERRY. This dock at Morrow Cove was the Vallejo departure point for the vessels of the Six Minute Ferry Company. The company was organized in 1919 and named for the brief duration of the trip across the Carquinez Straits to Crockett. The company also operated ferries between Vallejo and Mare Island. The Rodeo-Vallejo Ferry Company eventually took over the route, but went out of business following the completion of the Carquinez Bridge in 1927. Morrow Cove later became the home of the California Maritime Academy.

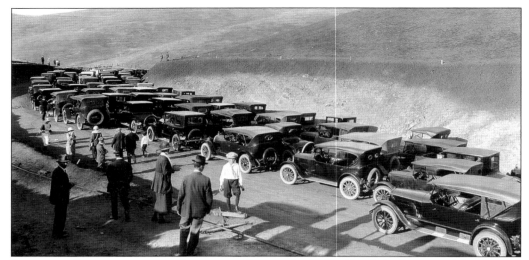

BREAKING GROUND FOR THE CARQUINEZ BRIDGE. In 1923 officials broke ground for the new Carquinez Bridge. So many local residents wanted to attend the event that their cars backed up in a massive traffic jam leading to Morrow Cove. The bridge was the brainchild of Aven J. Hanford and Oscar H. Klatt, operators of the Rodeo-Vallejo Ferry Company. The growth of automobile traffic had caused a ten-fold increase in the number of vehicles using their auto ferries in the five years from 1918 to 1923. The need for a bridge across the straits became obvious and the two partners formed the American Toll Bridge Company to undertake the project.

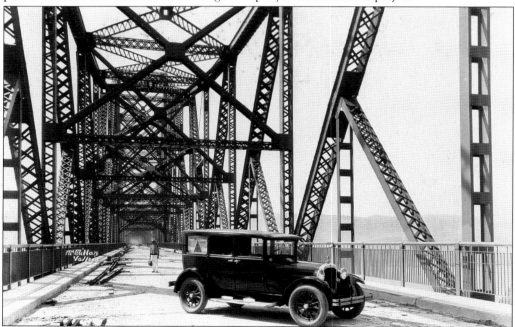

A SNEAK PREVIEW OF THE NEW BRIDGE. Although the Carquinez Bridge wasn't officially dedicated until May 21, 1927, on May 9 local automobile dealer George Dalwigk sneaked this brand new 1927 Dodge onto the span for a photograph. Dalwigk used the photo in an advertisement comparing the strength of the vehicles from his dealership with the strength of the massive new steel bridge.

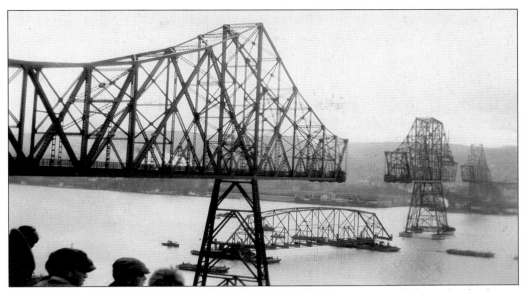

RAISING THE FINAL SPAN. These photos show the laborious process of lifting the final span section into place on the new Carquinez Bridge. On March 19, 1927, the final section was moved up the strait on barges. Massive counterweights were suspended from the already completed portions of the bridge and were slowly filled with sand. As their weight eventually increased to 750 tons each, the span was slowly hoisted on cables into position. This spectacular engineering feat was completed in less than an hour.

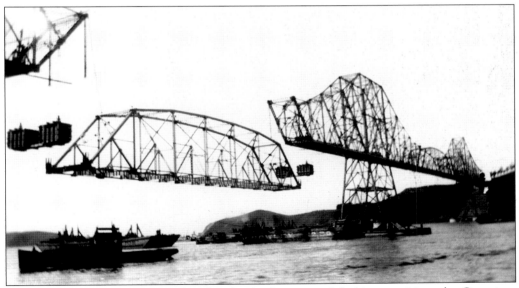

THE BRIDGE OPENS. Two months after the final span was lifted into position, the Carquinez Bridge officially opened. Thousands of people attended the ceremony on March 21, 1927. The governors of four states—California, Oregon, Washington, and Nevada—were on hand for the dedication. The great celebration was nearly eclipsed by other momentous news, shouted by newsboys hawking their afternoon papers on the bridge: American pilot Charles Lindbergh had reached Paris, completing the first solo trans-Atlantic airplane flight.

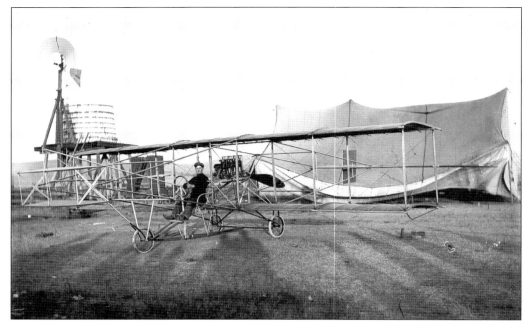

VALLEJO'S PIONEER AVIATORS. Pilot and airplane builder Rueben Coombs built Vallejo's first airplane with partner Paul Butler around 1910. The plane was made of bicycle parts, and the enterprising builders had a Grey Eagle engine shipped out from Kentucky to power the machine. Their early "airfield" was located on the Hann's Ranch, which today is the area at the end of Nebraska and Illinois Streets, near Interstate 80. Pilot Coombs is shown here with the plane.

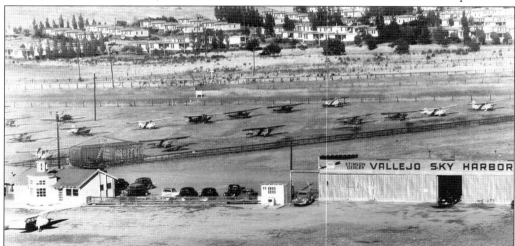

VALLEJO'S AIRPORTS. Vallejo has had several small airports, including Sky Harbor, pictured here, established just after World War II about two miles north of the city. Another of Vallejo's early landing fields was Knight's Airport, located near the present day intersection of Sacramento Street and Highway 37, where early day pilots often had to dodge jackrabbits scurrying across the landing strip. A further drawback was the fact that the field was frequently submerged under two to three feet of water after heavy winter rains. The Mini Airport was located near the intersection of Highway 37 and Broadway. Tall eucalyptus trees, still standing today, presented an interesting challenge for incoming pilots.

Six

VALLEJO SCHOOL DAYS

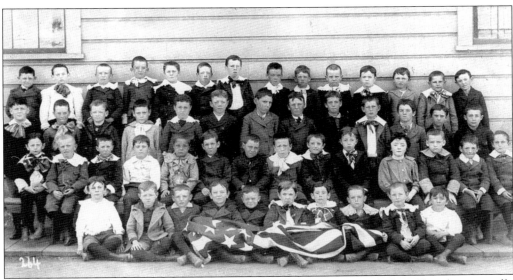

Vallejo Students at St. Vincent's School. St. Vincent's Catholic Church originally maintained separate schools for boys and girls. The 1898 boys class pictured here, from left to right, included: (first row) Raymond Ney, John Connolly, George O'Neal, John Salazar, Leo O'Neil, Ray McKenzie, Frank Falls, Harry Small, David Allen, John Kennedy, Jay Cunningham, Jimmy Powers, Frank Bade, and David Kelleher; (second row) Harry Brown, Willie Barne, Frank McSorley, John Allen, Fred Falls, David Flemming, George Narvall, Frank Bukes, John Riley, George Bade, Dan Sullivan, James Riley, and Leo Peoria; (third row) Joseph Clark, Rudy Hatt, George Glover, George Blanco, Eddie Barros, Charles McKerron, Leo Rutan, Walter Elvin, Joseph Brosnahan, Peter White, Willie Ryan, Bart Supple, Leo Jones, and Leo Cavanaugh; (fourth row) Charles Williams, James McGuire, Louis Jones, Bert Seymour, Harry Seymour, Joseph Sheean, Ray Palmer, Walter Smith, Fred Bade, and Joe Williams.

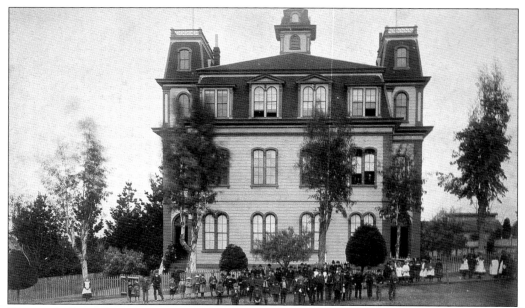

VALLEJO'S FIRST PUBLIC SCHOOL. The community's first public school built with citizen's tax money was located on Carolina Street near Sonoma Boulevard. Students in primary grades met on the lower levels and high school classes were held on the third floor. In 1870 the school had eight employees: six teachers, a janitor, and the principal. Their salaries ranged from $50 to $150 per month. The building was destroyed by an arson fire in 1894. The school is shown here in the spring of 1887.

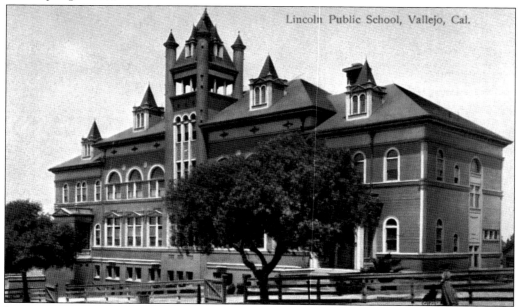

Lincoln Public School, Vallejo, Cal.

LINCOLN SCHOOL. Vallejo's Lincoln Public School was located on Carolina Street and today is the site of the Lincoln Elementary School. The huge Gothic Revival structure was built in 1894 and demolished in December 1938. The property was originally owned by Vallejo's founder, John Frisbie, and was donated to the city for the construction of the city's first public school.

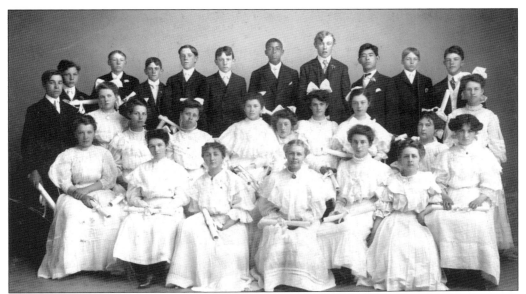

LINCOLN GRAMMAR SCHOOL CLASS OF 1905. The 27 members of the Lincoln Grammar School graduating class of 1905 pose for their class photo. Their class colors were orange and green and the class motto was "Strive to Succeed!" The boys in the class, from left to right, included George Willis, Reginald Venable, Louis Boss, Irwin Whitthorne, Homer Ashley, Earl Mitchell, Ellsworth Courtney, Frank Kelly, Sangora Ito, Walter Wilson, and Ray Bangle. The girls in the class, from left to right, were Ara Prentiss, Ethel Wetmore, Amelia Fowles, Elsa Bailar, Ruby Lambert, Pearl Lundquist, Anne Jeffers, Annie Wunnenberg, Gracie Dolan, Mamie Bulack, Myrtle Ross, Marie McPherson, Bertha Aden, Gertrude Winslow, Mamie Hagel, and Bessie Falls.

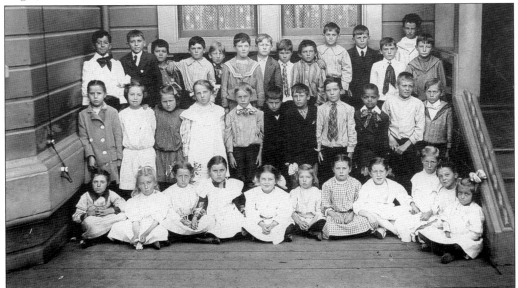

LINCOLN SCHOOL C. 1909. This third or fourth grade class at Lincoln School posed for their class photo around 1909. Note that the boys are all turned out in their snazzy neckties while the girls wear their finest hair ribbons.

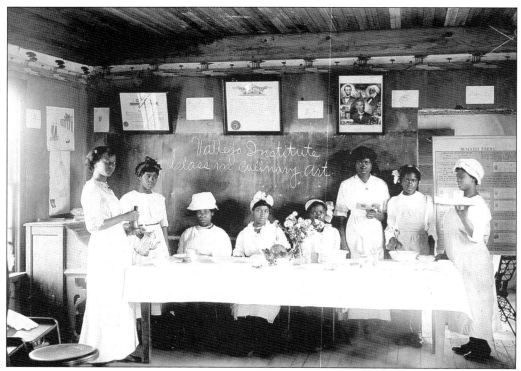

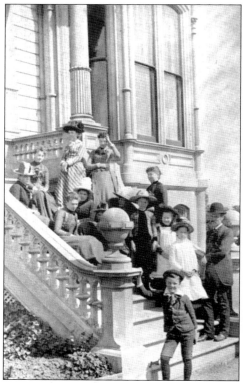

VALLEJO INDUSTRIAL AND NORMAL INSTITUTE. Charles H. Toney came to Vallejo from his home state of Texas in 1907. In 1911 he established the Vallejo Industrial and Normal Institute at 2100 Marin Street. The school stressed classroom education and job training for African-American students and was patterned after Booker T. Washington's famous Tuskegee Institute. Toney's institute provided classes and training for students in first through twelfth grades, and was the first school of its type in California. Ironically, the school was ordered closed in 1934 after Toney faced criticism for operating a segregated facility.

THE IRMA SCHOOL FOR YOUNG LADIES. The mansion formerly owned by John and Fannie Frisbie became the Irma School for Young Ladies after the Frisbies moved to Mexico. The school, located at the corner of Virginia and Sutter Streets, was headed by Prof. John M. Chase. In 1890 the two members of the Irma's first graduating class were Misses Rae Cassady and Jessie Harrier. The former Frisbie mansion later became the Vallejo Elks Club. It was destroyed by fire on New Years' Day, 1933.

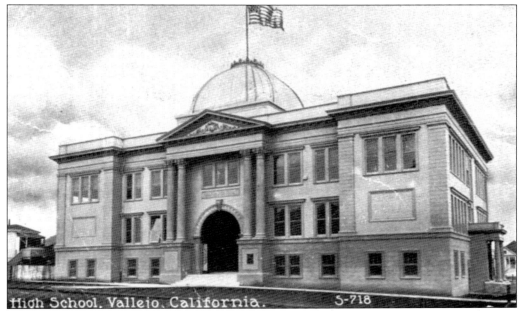

VALLEJO HIGH SCHOOL. In 1911, due to overcrowding at the old Lincoln Public School, a new Vallejo High School was built on Ohio Street. The school was dedicated on January 26, 1912 and served as Vallejo's high school for about ten years. It then became a junior high known as Washington School. After the school building was torn down, the location became Washington Park.

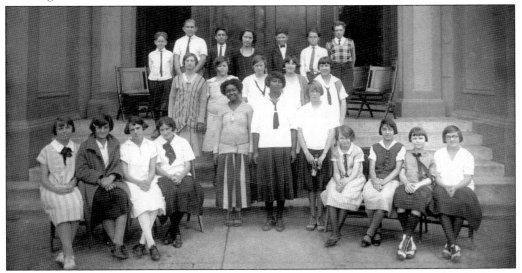

WASHINGTON JUNIOR HIGH. With the construction of a new high school on Nebraska Street, the old high school became Washington Junior High. Students in this 1924 class photo, from left to right, included: (front row) Madeline Jewett, Lorraine Vanderkarr, Aelodia Enos, Helen Gray (seated), unidentified, Mary Brown, Willa Wiggins (standing), Loretta Corcoran, Emily Moon, unidentified, and Miriam Barr (seated); (middle row) Edith Ottolini, unidentified, unidentified, Helen Sullivan, and Doris Clark; (back row) George Derr, Harold Rudstrom, Frank Frankos, teacher Muriel Knowles, Harold Almy, unidentified, and unidentified.

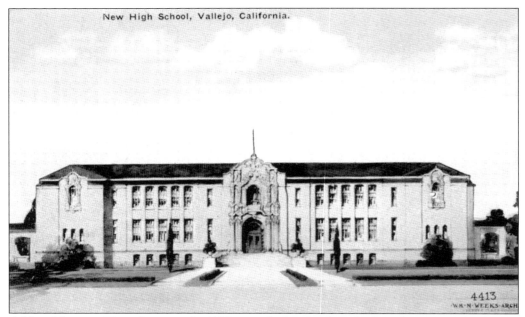

New High School, Vallejo, California.

4413
WM·N·WEEKS·ARCH

A NEW VALLEJO HIGH SCHOOL. In 1922 a new high school was built at the corner of Nebraska and Amador Streets. The new school, designed by architect William Weeks, was dedicated on April 15, 1922. Over the next 50 years, several new buildings were added to the high school campus. The main school building was closed in 1972 due to its failure to meet minimum earthquake safety standards. It was demolished in 1977.

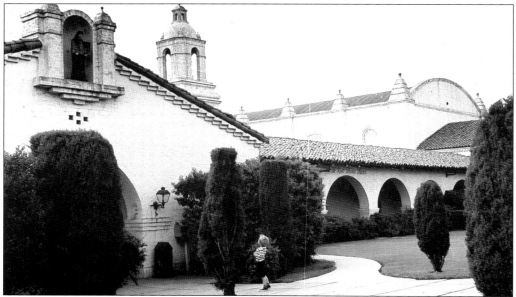

MARIANO G. VALLEJO JUNIOR HIGH SCHOOL. Built in 1933 and designed by San Francisco architect Frederick H. Reimers, this beautiful Mission Revival-style school featured distinctive mosaics and frescoes by artists Maxine Albro and Simeon Pelenc. The sculpture in a niche over the front entrance was said to represent Clio, the muse of history. The building was unable to conform to modern earthquake safety standards and was torn down in 1974.

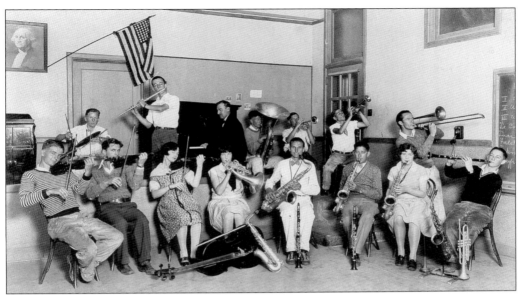

ALL THAT JAZZ. In 1928 the Vallejo High School Jazz Band was playing the cutting edge music of the era. Pictured, from left to right, are: (front row) Herman Freudenberg Jr., Al Lopez, Gladys Kemp, Miss Barton, Bob Moon, Eddie Martinez, Arvella Dickey, and Alvin Harris; (back row) Tom Eddington, Dick Shepard, teacher George Neill, John Austin, Morgan Wood, Henry Cassady, and Gene Gelling.

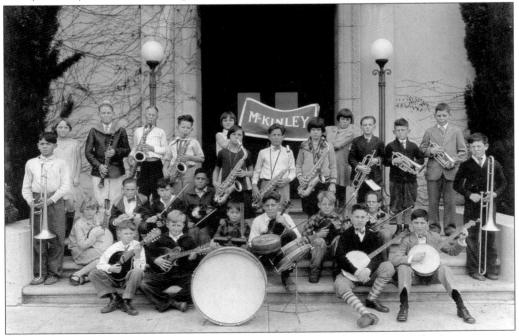

PLAYING IN THE BAND. Members of the McKinley School Orchestra pose at the front entrance of their school in this January 1928 photo. Music programs in Vallejo's schools have produced numerous talented musicians over the years. Many have gone on to enjoy successful professional careers.

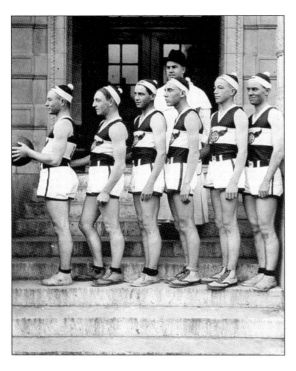

ST. VINCENT'S BASKETBALL TEAM. Members of the St. Vincent's High School basketball team pose in this undated photo. The growing number of students enrolled in Vallejo's Catholic school prompted the construction of a new school building in 1917. In the fall of 1918 the school was temporarily used as a community hospital during the influenza epidemic.

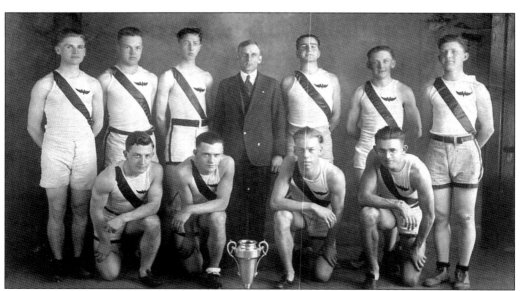

VALLEJO HIGH TRACK TEAM. One of Vallejo's most outstanding athletes was Elmer Boyden (front row, far right), a member of the 1920 Vallejo High School track team. Boyden represented Vallejo at the 1921 Annual Scholastic Track Meet at the University of Chicago where he won the 440- and 880-yard runs and the broad jump. Boyden Oval at Vallejo High School was named in his honor. Others in this picture, from left to right, included: (front row) Bill Topley, Justin "Tud" Collins, Alex Robertson, and Boyden; (back row) Cecil Lavers, Curtis Clark, Arvil Chappel, coach Elmer C. Neander, Ernest St. Martin, Ollie Ross, and Ross Capell.

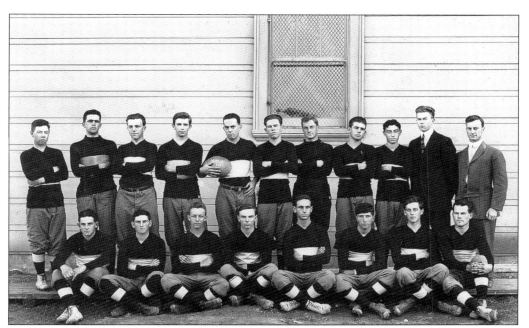

VALLEJO HIGH FOOTBALL TEAM, 1913. Several members of the Vallejo High School 1913 football team went on to become prominent civic and business leaders in the community. Team members, from left to right, included: (front row) unidentified, Jack Collins, Ainsworth Harvey, Rome Mini, Wilbur Green, Severus Mini, unidentified, and Earl Burns; (back row) Francis McDonald, Ben Cassidy, Kenneth Dick, Bill Hanley, Ray Luchsinger, Eugene McGrane, Carl Nielson, Fred Heegler, Babe Madrid, Chester Greenwood, and Professor Jackson.

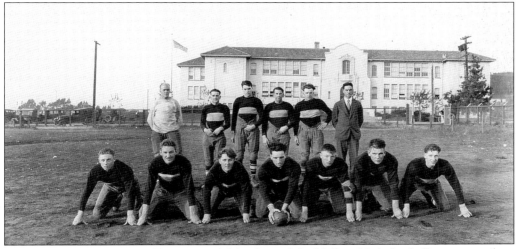

VALLEJO HIGH FOOTBALL TEAM, 1925. Members of the Vallejo High football team pose for a team photo on November 11, 1925. Three days after the photo was taken, Vallejo won the championship of the Northwest League of the California Interscholastic Federation by beating previously undefeated San Rafael High School 28-6. Vallejo team members, from left to right, included: (front row) Howard Rowe, "Mud" Howard, Bill Jones, Harvey Dahlgren, unidentified, Rodger Dennis, and Ken Welch; (back row) unidentified, Bill Wiggins, Bob Patterson, Dick Boyle, Guy Murray, and coach Colon Kilby.

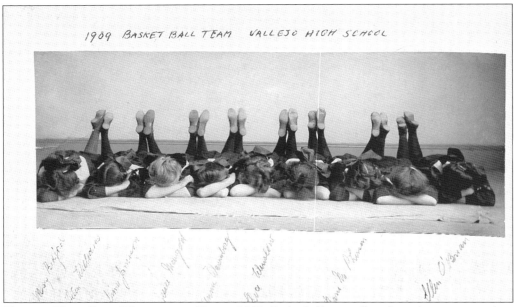

1909 BASKET BALL TEAM   VALLEJO HIGH SCHOOL

VALLEJO HIGH GIRLS' BASKETBALL TEAM, 1909. Basketball was still a relatively new sport when these members of the Vallejo High School girls' team clowned for the camera in 1909. In Vallejo, the sport was first played by girls' teams, though opponents from neighboring schools were often difficult to find. Boys' basketball wasn't organized at Vallejo High until 1912. Pictured here, from left to right, are Mary Bedford, Helen Williams, Irma Jamison, Jessie Mangold, Annie Wunnenberg, Elva Winslow, Marie McPherson, unidentified, and Ellen O'Brien.

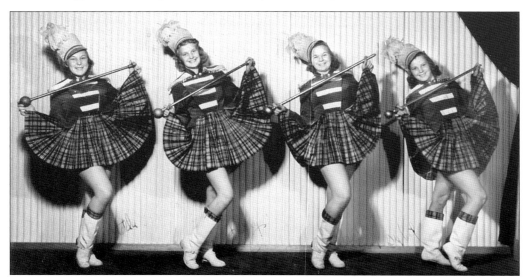

DRUM MAJORETTES. Vallejo High School Drum Majorettes practiced their steps for this 1940 photo. Pictured from left to right are Stella Wilson, unidentified, Sybil Cook, and Helen Rogers. The four majorettes and a division of flag girls appeared with the Vallejo High School Band under the direction of George F. Neill. In addition to football games and other school events, the ensemble also performed at the New Year's Day East-West Game at Kezar Stadium in San Francisco.

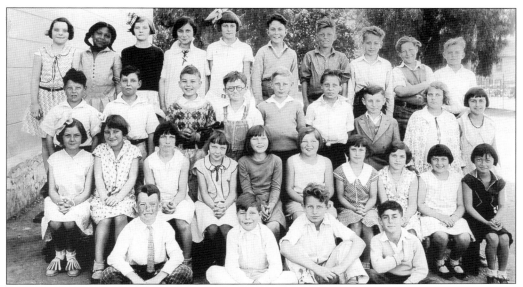

LINCOLN SCHOOL, C. 1928. Some of the members of this class from Lincoln Grammar School, from left to right, included Philip Ward, Fayette Hilton, Billy Stevens, Allen Larsen, Melvin Oden, Lucille Maritz, Ruth Behler, Julia Rhead, Ilahbel Weir, Roberta Clark, Carmel Bellini, Darralene Lewis, Lorraine Fong, Leigh Sparrow, Teddy Chancellor, George Hartzell, and Benton Meyer.

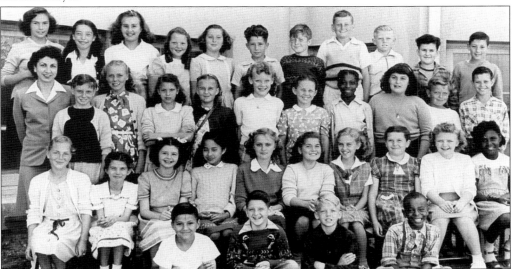

MCKINLEY SCHOOL, 1947. Students in Miss Rose Kalajian's fifth grade class at McKinley School pose for a photo in May 1947. Class members, from left to right, included: (first row) Donald Hill, Michael McNiel, LeRoy Blackwell, and Benny Toney; (second row) Dolores Bowker, Carmen Usiak, Roberta Milstead, Patricia Dacong, Virginia Philipps, Leah Bellettini, Barbara Ingalls, Eleanor Stevenson, Joan Silva, and Alberta Armstrong; (third row) Miss Kalajian, Jean Aitken, Carolyn Anderson, Velma Lee, Donna King, Glenda Odale, Jean Scott, Robbie Hicks, Angela ?, Richard King, and Richard Stacy; (fourth row) Charlotte Barger, Dorothy Cooley, Jeanne Hamilton, Joan Fisk, Carolyn Briggs, Billy Cowan, Gary Herbert, Edgar Boot, Jan Stedman, Ronald Avila, and Roger Corda.

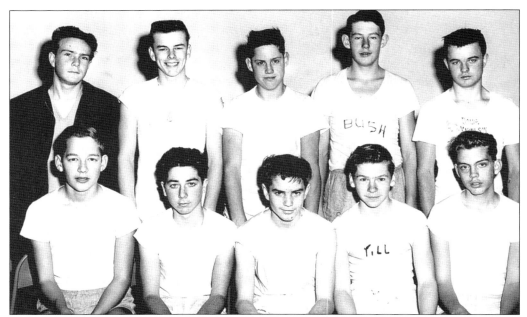

HOGAN JUNIOR HIGH SWIM TEAM. Members of the 1956 Hogan Junior High School swimming team, from left to right, included: (front row) Charles Kindig, Frank Bratt, Robert Dade, Eugene Till, and Robert Sather; (back row) David Sullivan, Stewart Reeves, James Shawhan, Charles Bush, and Douglas Mickelson. Not pictured is coach Joseph Norlin.

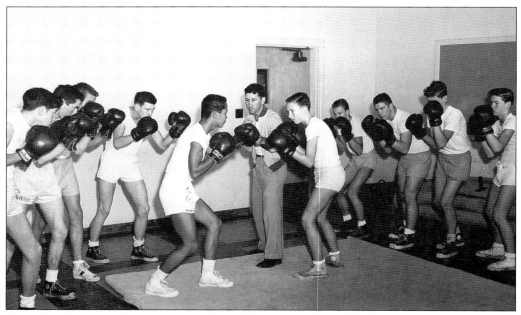

PHYS. ED. CLASS AT HOGAN JUNIOR HIGH. Members of this 1956 physical education class, from left to right, included Lewis Byram, Stan Brainard, Joe Keskeys, Ray Parsons, Tom Damian, W. Matthews, Keno De Varney, Jim Lamb, Bill Sage, Wayne Newgard, and Eugene Till. Hogan opened as a junior high school in 1953 and became Vallejo's second high school in 1962.

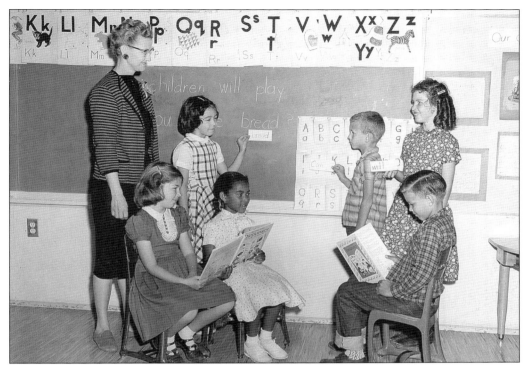

DAVIDSON ELEMENTARY SCHOOL, 1959. Teacher Polly Anna Day gives her students a spelling lesson in this April 1959 photo. Davidson Elementary School was named for John Davidson (1870-1951), a prominent local citizen who worked for 38 years at Mare Island and then served several terms on the Vallejo school board after his retirement. (Courtesy of Vallejo *Times-Herald*.)

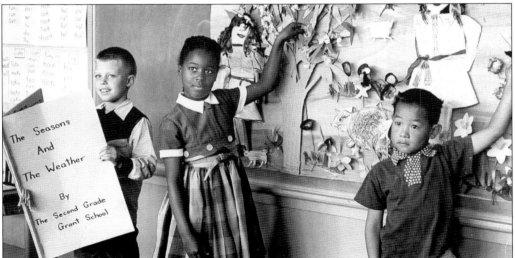

GRANT SCHOOL SECOND GRADERS. In April 1960 second grade students Dean Hadfield, Azellea Cooley, and Rey Mariano presented a report on "The Seasons and the Weather" at Grant Elementary School in South Vallejo. Grant School was one of Vallejo's earliest schools. The original school was built on Fifth Street in 1882. A newer Grant School was built across the street from the old school in 1922. (Courtesy of Vallejo *Times-Herald*.)

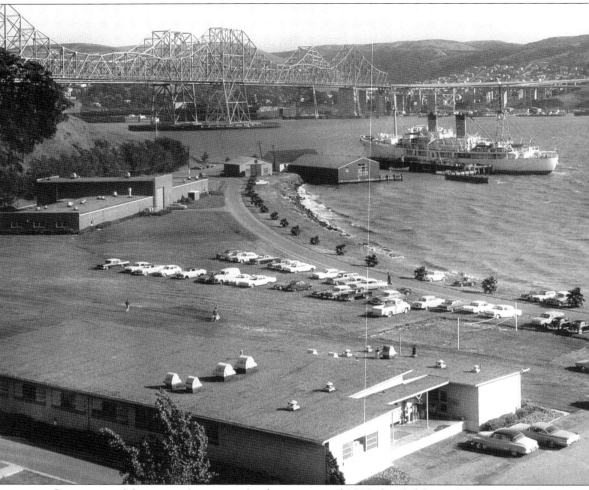

CALIFORNIA MARITIME ACADEMY. In the summer of 1943 the California Maritime Academy relocated from Tiburon to its new home at Morrow Cove in Vallejo. The academy provided training for students embarking on careers in the maritime industry. The original 67-acre site was expanded by partial filling of the cove, which was formerly the docking spot for the Six Minute Ferry Company. This photo shows the campus and the training ship *Golden Bear* around 1960.

Seven
VALLEJO GOES TO WAR!

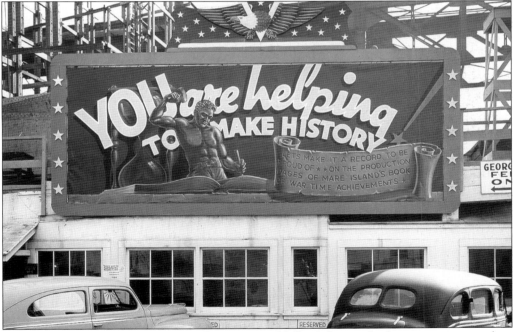

HELPING TO MAKE HISTORY. No other event in Vallejo's history had a greater impact than World War II. Mare Island played a critical role in the war effort as thousands of people labored around the clock building and repairing ships at the navy yard. Workers were urged to redouble their efforts with inspiring, patriotic banners like the one shown here, painted by artist Vladimir Shkurkin. Several ships built at Mare Island would gain near-legendary status for their heroic wartime exploits. Workers flocked to California to find employment at West Coast shipyards, and the result was unparalleled growth and change for cities like Vallejo.

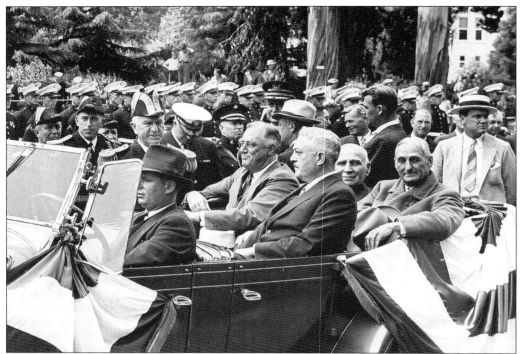

FDR VISITS MARE ISLAND, 1938. With war clouds gathering on the horizon in Europe, Mare Island Naval Shipyard began to gear up for the coming conflict. By the late 1930s the shipyard's workforce had increased to 20,000 people. In 1938 President Franklin Roosevelt made a tour of West Coast military installations to assess their preparedness for war. Roosevelt is shown here on his arrival at Mare Island on July 14. Congressman Frank Buck is seated to Roosevelt's left. In the back seat are Gov. Frank Merriam and U.S. Senator William Gibbs McAdoo.

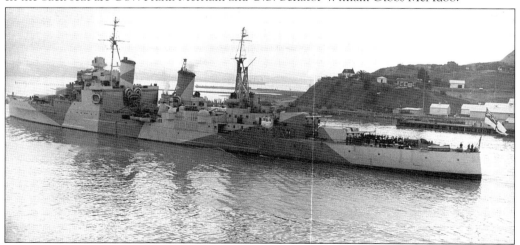

BRITISH VISITORS. The British cruiser *HMS Liverpool* came to Mare Island for repairs in 1941, before the United States officially entered World War II. *HMS Orion* also was repaired at Mare Island during the early days of the war. British sailors were welcomed warmly by local residents, even though their presence at Mare Island was officially a "secret." *HMS Liverpool* is shown here departing Mare Island on October 31, 1941. Five weeks later, the United States entered the war.

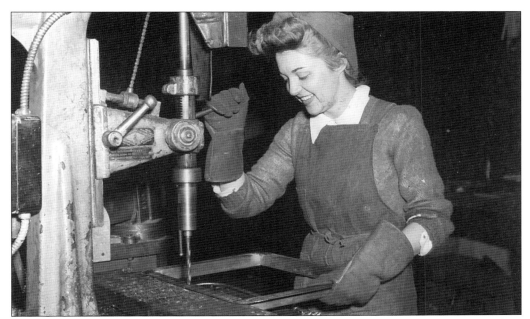

WOMEN DEFENSE WORKERS. After America's entry into World War II, Mare Island workers labored around the clock in support of the war effort. With many of the nation's men serving overseas in the navy, army and marine corps, women were called upon to undertake crucial wartime work. The popular image of "Rosie the Riveter" reflected the important role that women played during the war. Alice Hanneman, shown here, was one of the thousands of women who worked at Mare Island during World War II. At the height of the war, Mare Island employed close to 9,000 women. (Official U.S. Navy photo.)

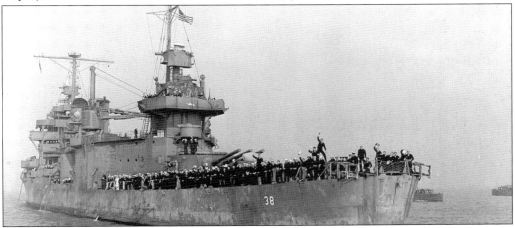

USS SAN FRANCISCO COMES HOME. Ships built at Mare Island played key roles in World War II. Among the most notable was the heavy cruiser *USS San Francisco*, launched at Mare Island in 1933. *USS San Francisco* was heavily damaged during the night battle of Guadalcanal on November 12-13, 1942. Rear Admiral Daniel Callaghan was among the 189 men killed or wounded in the action. Callaghan was the highest ranking naval officer killed in battle in U.S. history. *USS San Francisco* limped back to Mare Island for repairs and Admiral Callaghan was honored posthumously with the Medal of Honor. Vallejo's Admiral Callaghan Lane was named in his honor. (Official U. S. Navy photo.)

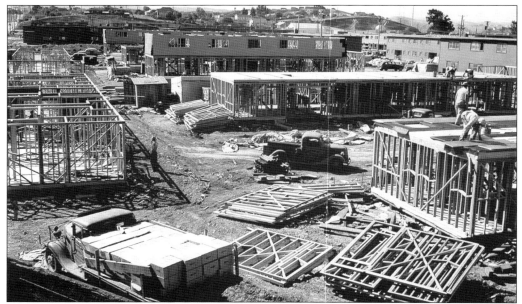

DEFENSE HOUSING UNDER CONSTRUCTION. Temporary defense housing projects sprang up almost overnight as people from nearly every state in the Union came seeking jobs at Mare Island. The city's population exploded from approximately 30,000 residents in 1939 to nearly 90,000 in 1945. Wartime housing projects were often built of prefabricated sections and used innovative building materials and techniques. Several well-known architects were involved in Vallejo's wartime housing boom, including William Wurster, who later became dean of the University of California Architecture School at Berkeley. (Official U.S. Navy photo.)

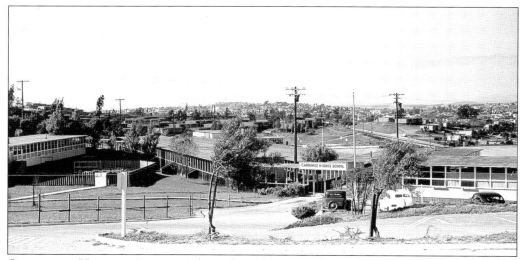

CARQUINEZ HEIGHTS SCHOOL. The influx of new residents into the city put demands on schools, businesses, transportation, health care, and other city services. New schools were built to accommodate the children of the city's growing workforce. Carquinez Heights School was built as part of the Carquinez Heights housing project in South Vallejo. Other schools built during the war included Highland, Federal Terrace, Olympic and Steffan Manor Elementary Schools, and Franklin Junior High School. Courtesy of Vallejo *Times-Herald*.)

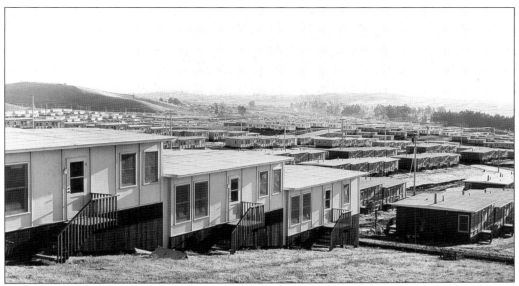

CHABOT TERRACE. By far the largest of Vallejo's defense housing projects was Chabot Terrace, located north of present day Highway 37 and east of Broadway. By late 1944 nearly 11,000 people were living in this project. Other wartime housing projects in Vallejo included Federal Terrace, Roosevelt Terrace, Guadalcanal Village, Carquinez Heights, Floyd Terrace, Hillside Dormitories, Northside Dormitories, Amador Apartments, Solano Apartments, and Victory Apartments. Nearly all of these were torn down soon after the war ended.

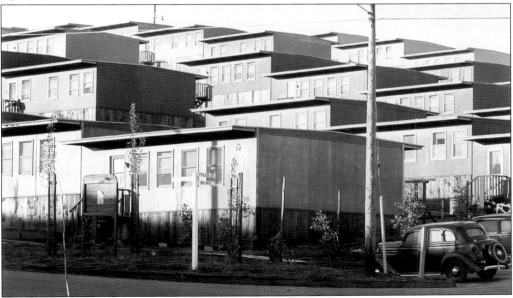

WARTIME GROWTH AND CHANGE. In 1945 a report by the City of Vallejo declared that the city had "undergone one of the most radical changes of any community in America in the past four years. Nowhere else has the impact of the war, with all of its resultant confusion, congestion, and expansion been more direct." Many families who lived in Vallejo's temporary defense housing projects later built or bought their own homes in the community. Others returned to their home states once the war had ended.

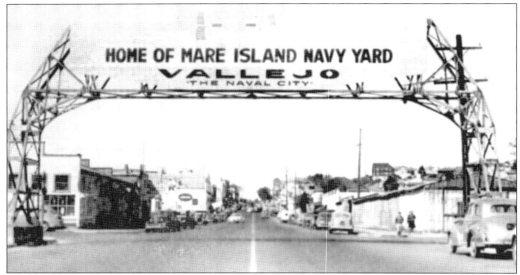

WELCOME TO VALLEJO! This arch across Sonoma Boulevard welcomed visitors to Vallejo in the 1940s. Activity at Mare Island kept Vallejo's downtown streets busy night and day. As early as May 1941, Mare Island's workforce had been expanded to 24 hours a day, seven days a week. As a result, many downtown Vallejo businesses stayed open around the clock to serve the needs of their customers.

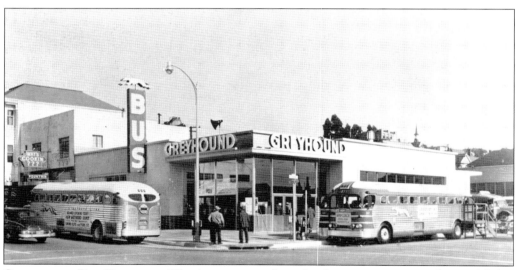

GREYHOUND BUS TERMINAL. Wartime rationing brought about restrictions on the availability of gasoline, tires, and automobiles. As a result, many newcomers to Vallejo during World War II got their first glimpse of the community when they arrived at the old Greyhound Bus Terminal at the corner of York Street and Sonoma Boulevard. During the war the navy also had a bus system, operating 300 buses to bring in workers from surrounding communities.

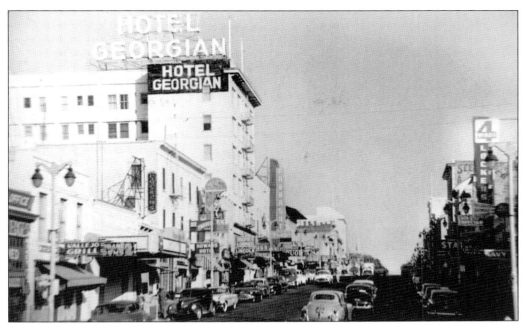

LOWER GEORGIA STREET. The bustling 200 block of Georgia Street is shown here in the 1940s. The eight-story Hotel Georgian was then Vallejo's tallest building. As the busy main street of a prosperous navy town, lower Georgia Street gained a notorious reputation for its many taverns, gaming parlors, and other businesses catering to the needs of adventurous sailors. This colorful section of town was demolished in the early 1960s.

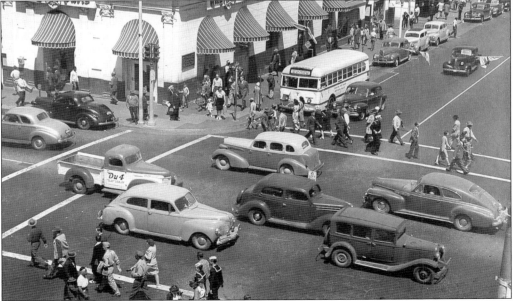

THE CENTER OF TOWN. This photo shows the crowded intersection of Georgia and Marin Streets during the 1940s. The popular City of Paris Department Store, one of San Francisco's most fashionable retailers, opened its first branch location in Vallejo in 1943. The tremendous increase in Vallejo's population during the war assured a robust downtown business scene.

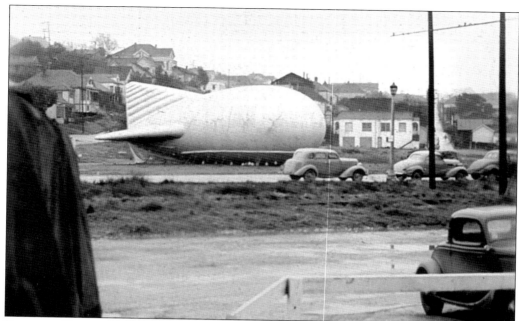

BARRAGE BALLOONS. During the war, barrage balloons were deployed throughout the city. Their purpose was to entangle and confuse low flying aircraft in the event of an enemy attack. This photo shows a barrage balloon sitting on the ground along Vallejo's waterfront although usually the hydrogen-filled balloons were tethered on lines high above the city. Occasionally one of the balloons would break loose or explode. One such explosion at Federal Terrace killed one person and injured 17 others.

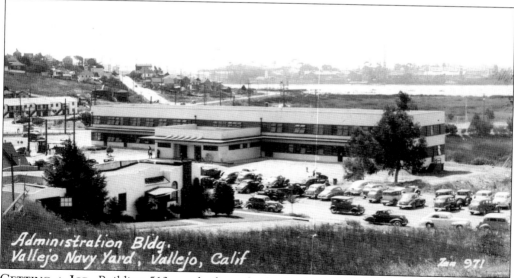

GETTING A JOB. Building 513 was built at the beginning of World War II as Mare Island's employment office, when thousands of defense workers were flocking to Vallejo in search of shipbuilding jobs. The employment office was located at the corner of Wilson Avenue and Tennessee Street, near Mare Island's main gate. At its peak, Mare Island employed nearly 50,000 workers during World War I

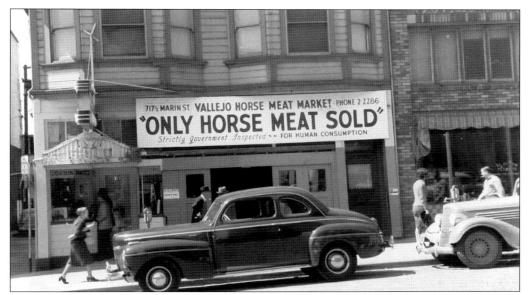

WARTIME RATIONING. Due to shortages and meat rationing during the war, the federal government authorized the sale of horse meat for human consumption. Melvin Rossi opened the Vallejo Horse Meat Market at 717 1/2 Marin Street in March 1943. Although Vallejo Mayor Jack Stewart declared "no one is going to eat horse meat if I can help it," he was overruled by other city council members, who approved the opening of the store.

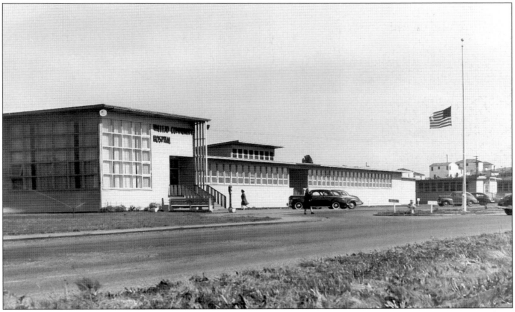

HEALTH CARE FOR DEFENSE WORKERS. The Vallejo Community Hospital was established during World War II to meet the needs of the thousands of civilian defense workers employed at Mare Island. The hospital was located on Napa Road, now Broadway, just south of the Floyd Terrace defense housing project. Vallejo Community Hospital later became part of the Kaiser Permanente system.

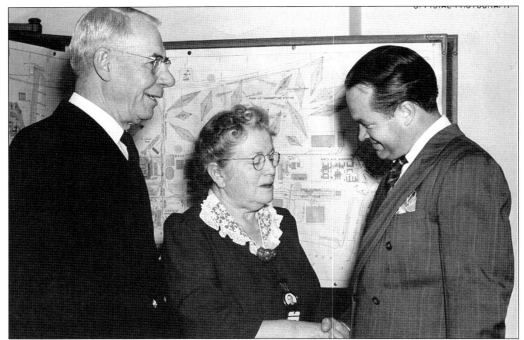

BOB HOPE VISITS. Actor and comedian Bob Hope visited Mare Island on December 7, 1943. Hope is shown here talking with Mare Island employee Ella Thomas David, bringing news of her son, Colonel Leon T. David, whom he had met in North Africa. During the war many actors, entertainers, and public figures visited Mare Island to boost worker morale. Among these visitors were Shirley Temple, Basil Rathbone, Eleanor Roosevelt, Hattie McDaniel, Jack Dempsey, Alistair Cooke, Bill "Bojangles" Robinson, and John Garfield. (Official U.S. Navy photo.)

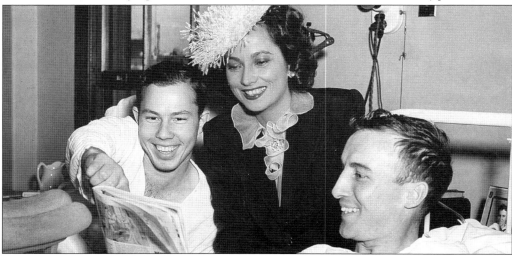

MERLE MEETS BOYS. Hollywood actress Merle Oberon visited wounded sailors at the Mare Island Naval Hospital in June 1943. Following the attack on Pearl Harbor in December 1941, the Mare Island Hospital treated wounded sailors evacuated from Hawaii. The hospital later made significant advances in the development of artificial limbs and prosthetic devices. (Official U.S. Navy photo.)

110

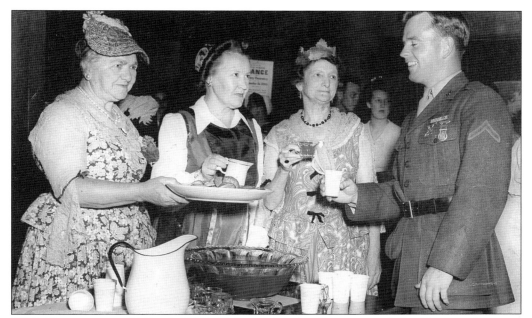

USO HOSPITALITY. Vallejo's USO Club on Amador Street provided soldiers, sailors, and marines with a welcomed touch of hospitality during World War II. In this photo, members of the Vallejo International Club Isabella Stark, Helga Anderson, and Annie Martin serve a glass of punch to Private Arthur S. Miller, USMC, during a July 1944 dance at the club. Jimmie Emerson's Orchestra provided the evening's entertainment. A second USO club was located on Georgia Street.

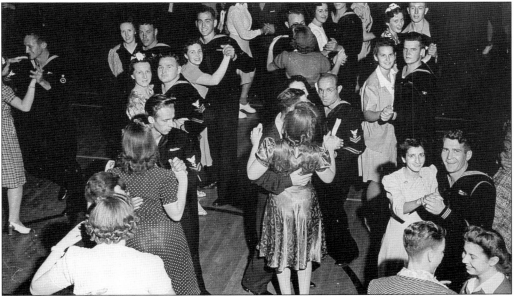

A DANCE AT THE NAVAL YMCA. During the war the Naval YMCA on Santa Clara Street sponsored dances for servicemen in conjunction with the USO. The YMCA was a "home away from home" for servicemen stationed at Mare Island. The facility included a swimming pool, gymnasium, auditorium, billiards room, library, bowling alley, and restaurant.

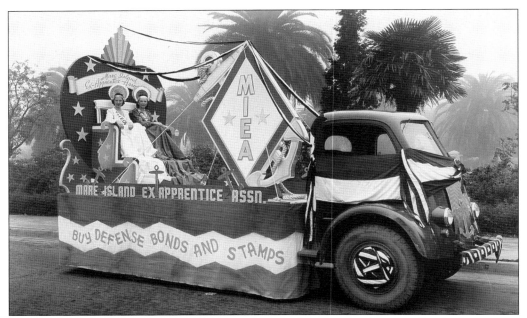

BOND RALLIES AND PARADES. Vallejoans were urged to support the war effort by buying war bonds. Bond rallies in Vallejo and at Mare Island often featured popular entertainers encouraging those in attendance to purchase bonds. Local movie theaters offered free admission with each bond sold. Patriotic parades featured colorfully decorated floats, like this float sponsored by the Mare Island Ex-Apprentice Association.

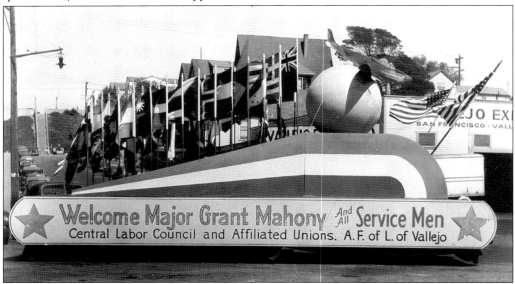

WELCOMING A HOMETOWN HERO. Vallejo native Colonel Grant Mahoney was given a tumultuous welcome and a spectacular parade when he returned home for a brief visit in July 1943. Mahoney received the Distinguished Service Cross for shooting down numerous enemy aircraft in the Pacific and Asian theaters and gained national publicity for his wartime heroism. But like so many other young men during World War II, Mahoney's luck ran out. He died when his plane was shot down in early 1945.

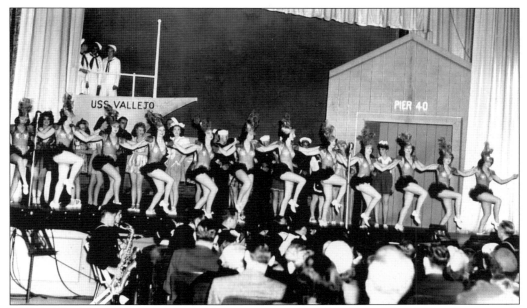

MIRA. The Mare Island Recreation Association was founded during World War II to provide entertainment and recreation for the thousands of sailors and civilian workers at the shipyard. This chorus line performed in a MIRA production called the Mare Island Follies of 1944. In addition to patriotic shows like the Mare Island Follies, MIRA also sponsored basketball, baseball, softball, golf, and bowling teams, in addition to groups like stamp clubs. The organization later evolved into the MIRA Theater Guild.

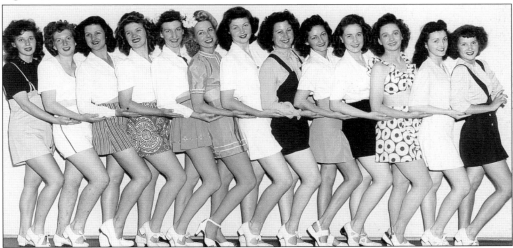

MARE ISLAND FOLLIES OF 1945. Mare Island's Adair Rhythmettes, under the direction of J. Mills Adair, performed in the Mare Island Follies of 1945. The Hollywood-style patriotic extravaganza held at Vallejo Junior High School featured singing, dancing, humorous skits, and musical production numbers. Most of the Rhythmettes also held day jobs performing vital defense work at the shipyard. Pictured here from left to right are Betty McCanless, Bernice Bregman, Mary Firtko, Clara Ortega, Helen Ochs, Cozette Ochs, Betty Johnson, Mary Drugas, Joanne Emerson, Ann Nicholson, Kay Flint, Cleo Wood, and Joanne McCanless. (Official U. S. Navy photo.)

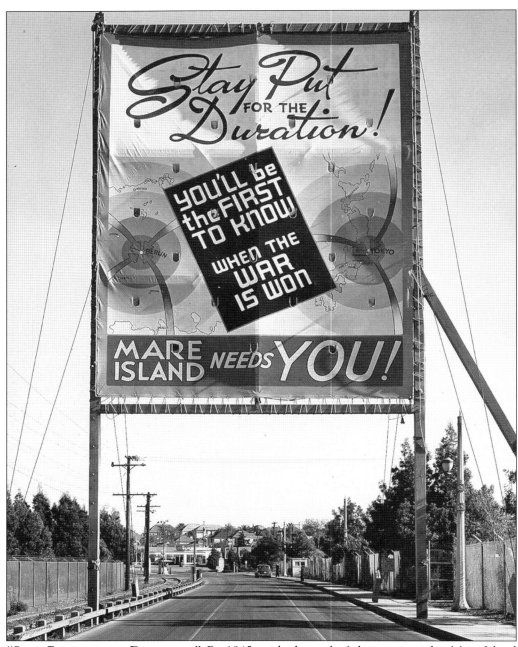

"Stay Put for the Duration." By 1945, with the end of the war in sight, Mare Island workers were urged to stick with their jobs until their efforts were successful. This large banner was erected near the shipyard's main gate to remind workers of the important task yet to be completed. In the summer of 1945, components of the atomic bomb were shipped out of Mare Island aboard the cruiser *USS Indianapolis*. When the news of Japan's surrender was announced, joyful celebrations erupted on the streets of downtown Vallejo. Mare Island workers had played a crucial role in World War II and the war brought about tremendous growth and significant changes for the City of Vallejo.

Eight
POST-WAR CHANGES
1946–1975

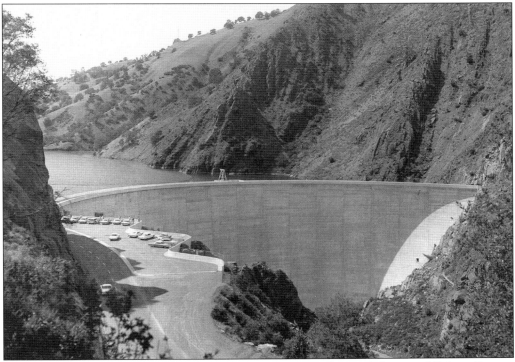

MONTICELLO DAM. In the years following World War II, Vallejo and the rest of Solano County experienced unprecedented growth. To ensure adequate water for the thriving region, the Solano Irrigation District was formed to develop plans for a dam on Putah Creek. The dam gained approval from the Department of the Interior and the Bureau of Reclamation, and groundbreaking ceremonies were held on September 25, 1953. At the ceremony, Gov. Earl Warren commented that "every month 30,000 people are coming to California, and not one of them brings a gallon of water." The Monticello Dam was completed in November 1957.

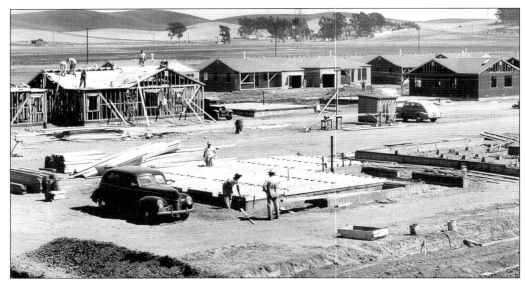

POST-WAR HOUSING BOOM. Vallejo experienced a building boom following World War II as new subdivisions sprang up on land formerly used for dairy farming. When these two- and three-bedroom homes in Vallejo Manor were completed in the summer of 1949 their prices ranged from $7,840 to $8,740. Vallejo also began to annex much of the unincorporated land surrounding the city, greatly expanding the size of the community. (Courtesy of Vallejo *Times-Herald*.)

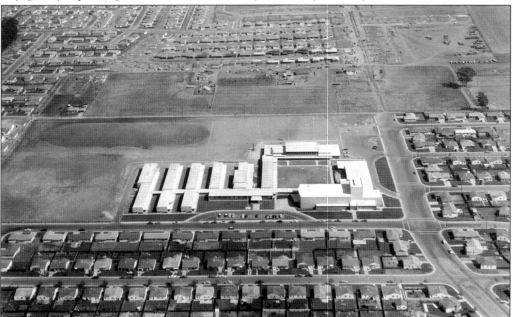

NEW SCHOOLS FOR A GROWING POPULATION. The opening of Hogan Junior High School in 1953 reflected Vallejo's post-war expansion. In 1962 Hogan became the city's second high school. Other schools built in the 1950s and early 1960s to accommodate the city's booming population included Cave Elementary (1953), Cooper Elementary (1954), Davidson Elementary (1956), Mare Island Elementary (1953), Mini Elementary (1962), Pennycook Elementary (1957), Solano Junior High (1962), and Springstowne Junior High (1962).

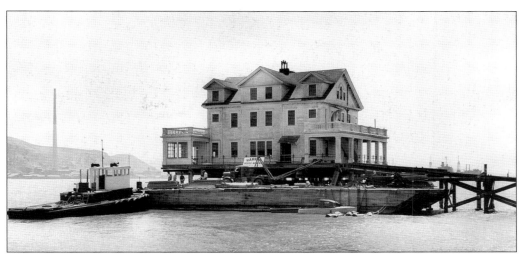

MOVING THE CARQUINEZ STRAIT LIGHTHOUSE. In 1955 workers from Hanna's House Moving Company prepared for the Herculean task of moving the old U.S. Coast Guard Carquinez Straits lighthouse to its new home at Elliot Cove. The three-story, 28-room lighthouse was built in 1910 and stood at the end of a long pier near the entrance to the straits, just off Sandy Beach. (Courtesy of Vallejo *Times-Herald*.)

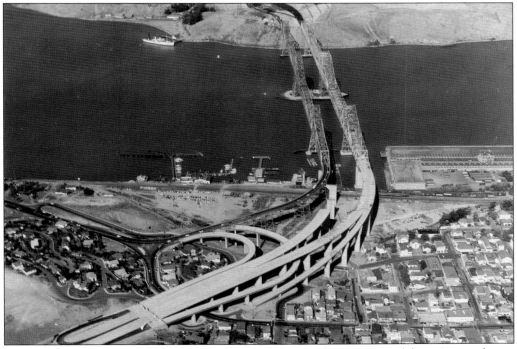

BRIDGING THE STRAITS. . . AGAIN. Following World War II, California's population continued to boom. The nation's interstate highway system expanded in response to America's increasing dependence on the automobile. In 1958 a second bridge was built across the Carquinez Straits, parallel to the 1927 span. Following World War II, the toll for crossing the original bridge had been eliminated. When the new bridge opened on November 25, 1958, tolls were reintroduced at 25 cents per car.

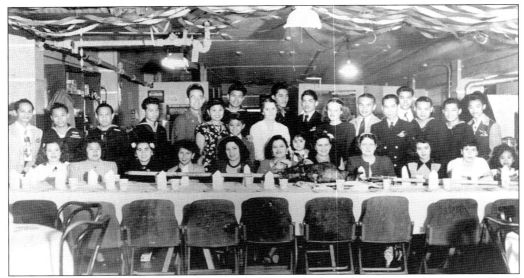

FILIPINO COMMUNITY CENTER. Changes in immigration laws allowed an increasing number of Filipinos to come to the United States following World War II. With its Filipino community already well established, Vallejo was a natural destination for many of these new immigrants. The Filipino Community Center was the hub of social life among Vallejo's Filipinos. This October 1946 photo shows a dinner honoring Filipino military veterans. At that time the center was located on Georgia Street, but it later moved to a new home on Sonoma Boulevard.

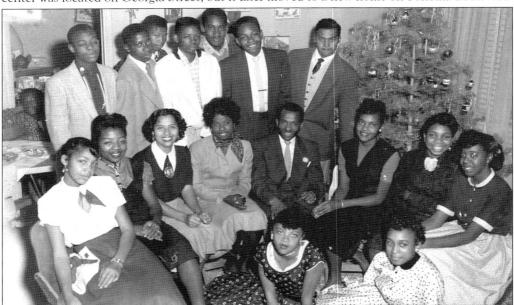

HAPPY HOLIDAYS, 1954. Members of the Youth Crusade, led by Rev. B. A. Williams, celebrated Christmas 1954, with a party at the home of Miss Edna Dickson. Pictured here , from left to right are: (seated in front row) Ovetta Birden and Ruth Hunt; (middle row) Loretta Hunt, Alazee Pierce, Jimmie Johnson, Artimae August, Rev. Williams, Edna Dickson, Myrtle Hunt, and Easter MacWilliams; (back row) Edward Brown, Herald August, Edward Anderson, Felix Woodson, Wallace Sheppard, Harry Henderson, and Gent Davis.

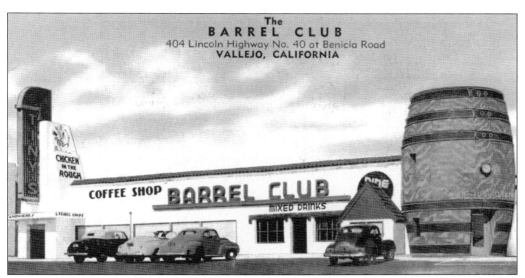

The

BARREL CLUB

404 Lincoln Highway No. 40 at Benicia Road
VALLEJO, CALIFORNIA

THE BARREL CLUB. A local landmark for many years, the Barrel Club was established in 1938 on old Highway 40 near Benicia Road. The popular restaurant and nightspot brought in top name entertainers from across the country. The distinctive barrel design was a familiar feature that welcomed many visitors to Vallejo, particularly during World War II. The Barrel Club was operated by the Curtola family until it was torn down in 1964.

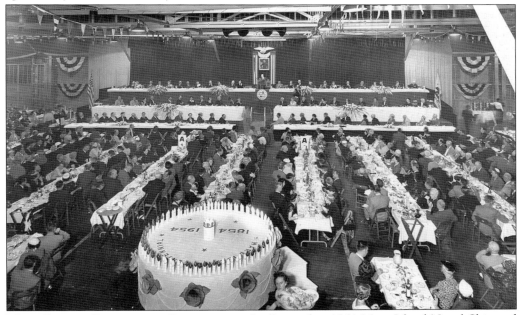

MARE ISLAND CENTENNIAL CELEBRATION. In September 1954 Mare Island Naval Shipyard celebrated its 100th birthday. More than 3,000 people attended the centennial banquet that was presided over by Master of Ceremonies Ed Sullivan. All of Vallejo celebrated the anniversary with parades, pageants, and community-wide festivities. The highlight of the banquet was the announcement by Admiral Robert B. Carney that Mare Island had been selected to participate in the navy's new nuclear submarine construction program. (Official U. S. Navy photo.)

119

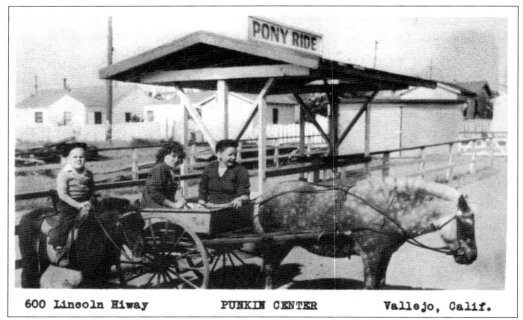

600 Lincoln Hiway   PUNKIN CENTER   Vallejo, Calif.

FAMILY FUN AT "PUNKIN' CENTER." Located on the east side of old Highway 40, just south of Georgia Street, "Punkin' Center" was a popular family destination in the 1940s and '50s. Children could enjoy pony rides, kiddie cars, and a merry-go-round. Highway 40 was replaced by Interstate 80 in the early 1960s.

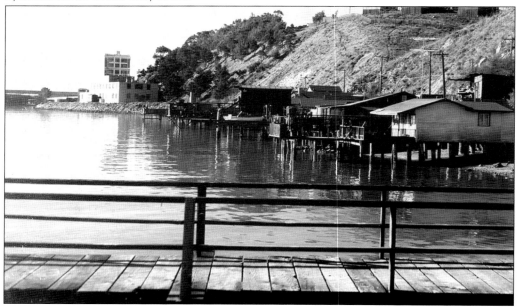

LIVING ON THE EDGE. Sandy Beach, shown here in 1952, is a unique neighborhood perched on the edge of the Carquinez Straits. The area originally was settled by Greek and Portuguese fishermen, but later developed a more eclectic mix of residents. People who live at "the beach" have a close bond, united by their isolation and their love for this beautiful neighborhood. (Courtesy of Vallejo *Times-Herald*.)

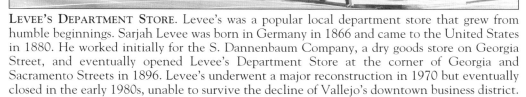

LEVEE'S DEPARTMENT STORE. Levee's was a popular local department store that grew from humble beginnings. Sarjah Levee was born in Germany in 1866 and came to the United States in 1880. He worked initially for the S. Dannenbaum Company, a dry goods store on Georgia Street, and eventually opened Levee's Department Store at the corner of Georgia and Sacramento Streets in 1896. Levee's underwent a major reconstruction in 1970 but eventually closed in the early 1980s, unable to survive the decline of Vallejo's downtown business district.

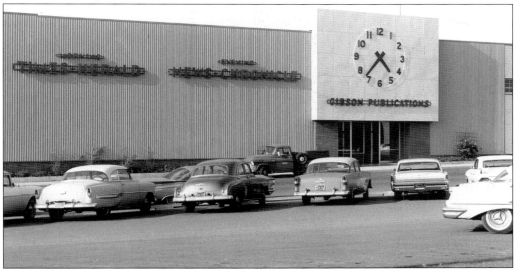

GIBSON PUBLICATIONS AND VALLEJO'S NEWSPAPERS. Shown here in the mid-1950s, Gibson Publications on Maryland Street, now Curtola Parkway, printed the Vallejo *Times Herald* and *Evening Chronicle*. Luther Gibson, who came to Vallejo from Santa Cruz in 1919, began publishing the Vallejo *Herald* in 1922 and soon thereafter bought the Vallejo *Times*, combining the two papers into the *Times-Herald*. Later, he bought and consolidated the Vallejo *Chronicle* and the Vallejo *News*. In 1948 Gibson was elected to the first of five terms in the California State Senate.

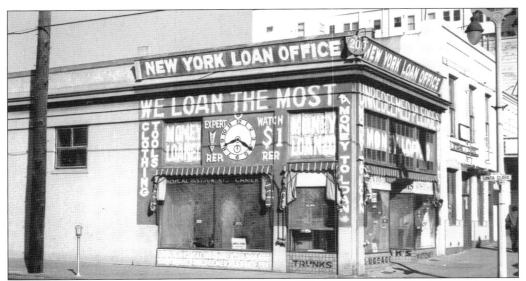

DOWNTOWN VALLEJO'S DECLINE. In the years following World War II it became apparent that Vallejo's 100-year-old downtown area was showing signs of age and decline. The city's 1957 master plan described the city's core as "a transitional area characterized by extreme age with little maintenance, general dilapidation, lack of compliance with existing building, plumbing, electrical, health, and housing codes, . . . lack of adequate streets, [and] lack of recreation areas."

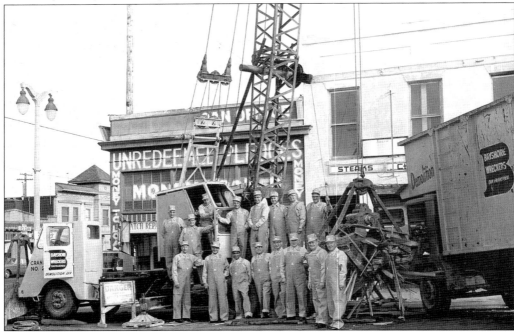

REDEVELOPMENT. The Vallejo Redevelopment Agency was established in 1956 to oversee the revitalization of the historic core of the city's downtown. City fathers envisioned a huge new development of stores, restaurants, a new post office, new city hall, a civic auditorium, a library, parking areas, a hotel/motel complex, pedestrian walkways, and a major waterfront freeway linking Highway 40 with the Sears Point Road. (Courtesy of Vallejo *Times-Herald*.)

"OUT WITH THE OLD. . ." The Marina
Vista Redevelopment Project encompassed
24 square blocks of commercial, residential,
and open space in downtown Vallejo. The
redevelopment agency acquired nearly 125
acres and began to demolish Vallejo's
historic old downtown in the name of
progress. In the early 1960s scores of
blighted and dilapidated buildings were torn
down. Unfortunately, a number of Vallejo's
most significant historic landmarks also
were demolished in this mammoth urban
renewal project. Among them were the old
Naval YMCA, the Carnegie Library, the
Astor House, the Lynch Building, and the
Vallejo Women's Club. (Courtesy of Vallejo
Times-Herald.)

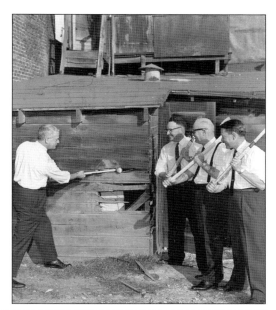

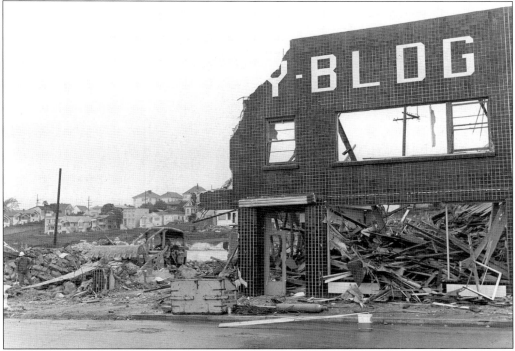

THE WRECKING BALL. Block after block of old downtown Vallejo was demolished during the
city's massive downtown redevelopment project. Not only buildings, but the very land itself was
transformed. The marshy waterfront area was developed into a seawall and pedestrian
promenade. The prominent York Street hill, where the old state capitol building once stood,
was graded out of existence. Blocks of former commercial buildings became parking lots and the
heart of the downtown neighborhood was cut off from the waterfront through a series of street
closures. (Courtesy of Vallejo *Times-Herald.*)

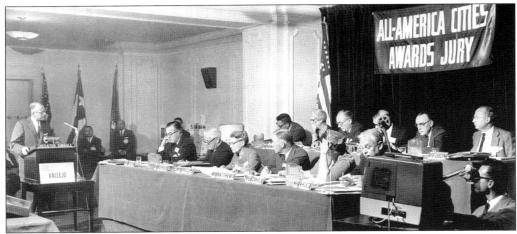

AN ALL-AMERICA CITY. In 1959 Vallejo received the prestigious All- America City Award from *Look* magazine. Vallejo attorney Henry Kilpatrick (left, at podium) presented Vallejo's case before the All- America City jury in Springfield, Massachusetts, on November 18, 1959. A contingent of 23 Vallejoans made the cross-country trip to Springfield to promote Vallejo before the judging panel. Vallejo was selected in recognition of its successful annexation program and its ambitious downtown/waterfront redevelopment project.

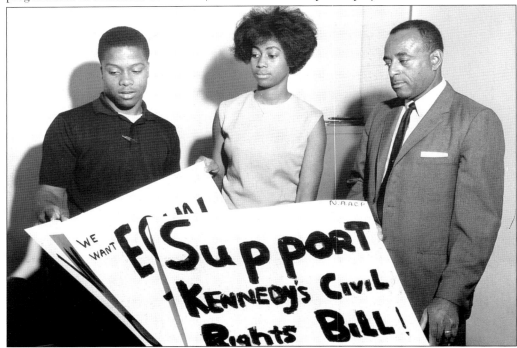

EYES ON THE PRIZE. African Americans in Vallejo joined the nationwide struggle for civil rights in the 1960s. On August 28, 1963, marchers assembled at Vallejo's waterfront park to support President Kennedy's civil rights bill. On the same day, in Washington D. C., 250,000 Americans gathered as Rev. Martin Luther King delivered his famous "I Have A Dream" speech. Shown here preparing for the Vallejo march are, from left to right, James Bircher, Patricia Jones, and DuWane Hill. (Courtesy of Vallejo *Times-Herald.*)

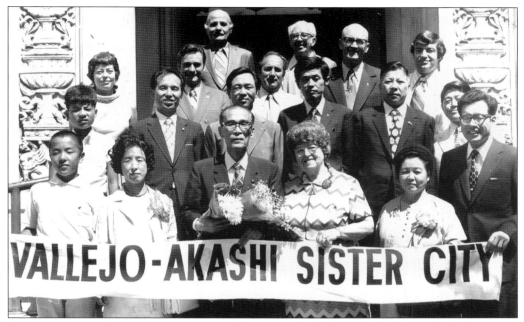

VALLEJO SISTER CITY ASSOCIATION. A delegation from Vallejo's Sister City of Akashi, Japan, poses with Vallejo Mayor Florence Douglas on the front steps of city hall in this July 1973 photo. The Sister City Association was established in 1971 to foster cultural exchanges between Vallejo and other cities around the world. Vallejo has established sister cities on nearly every continent.

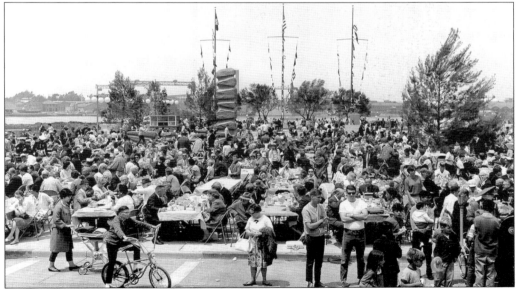

MARINA VISTA TOWN SQUARE DEDICATION. On June 4, 1967, Vallejoans celebrated the completion of the ambitious Marina Vista redevelopment project with the dedication of the town square at the foot of Georgia Street. The civic plaza featured monuments, commemorative plaques, and public sculptures, including artist Gordon Newell's massive granite sculpture *Silent Company*, shown here towering over the assembled crowd. (Courtesy of Vallejo *Times-Herald*.)

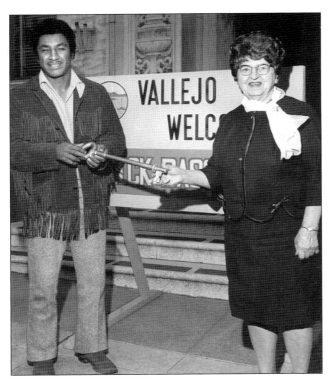

FOOTBALL GREAT DICK BASS. A 1955 graduate of Vallejo High School, Dick Bass went on to an impressive professional football career with the Los Angeles Rams. At Vallejo High, Bass was a member of the undefeated 1954 team, considered one of the best teams in the school's history. Bass scored an amazing 442 points in just 18 games and scored 30 or more points in a single game eight times. As a professional, Bass played in three pro bowls. In this 1970 photo, Bass receives the Key to the City from Vallejo Mayor Florence Douglas.

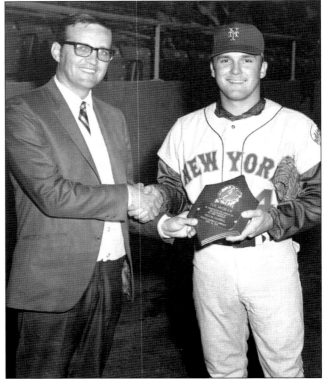

"YOU GOTTA BELIEVE!" Major League Baseball pitcher Tug McGraw played 19 seasons with the New York Mets and Philadelphia Phillies. The popular reliever and screwball specialist is remembered for his motto "you gotta believe" while playing for the 1973 National League champion Mets. Born and raised in Vallejo, McGraw was an outstanding athlete at St. Vincent's High School and Solano Junior College. He is shown here receiving a 1970 award "for loyalty to and recognition of his home community: Vallejo, California."

EPISCOPAL CHURCH FIRE.
Several of Vallejo's historic buildings were intentionally demolished in the early 1960s but, sadly, one cherished landmark fell victim to fire. The Ascension Episcopal Church on Georgia Street was destroyed by a blaze on July 24, 1969. The church was one of Vallejo's oldest buildings, constructed in 1867. Although the structure was a total loss, the congregation soon built a new church on Tuolumne Street. (Courtesy of Vallejo *Times Herald.*).

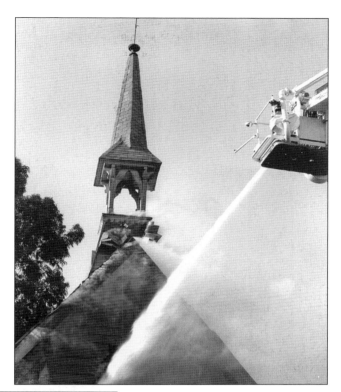

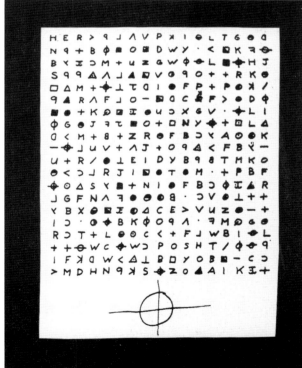

THE ZODIAC KILLER. In the late 1960s the City of Vallejo and the rest of the bay area were gripped by a series of tragic and bizarre murders. The killer referred to himself as the Zodiac in a number of taunting coded letters to local newspapers and law enforcement officials. In Vallejo, murders occurred on Lake Herman Road and at Blue Rock Springs. It has long been thought that the killer was probably a Vallejoan, although the case officially remains unsolved. (Courtesy of Vallejo *Times-Herald.*)

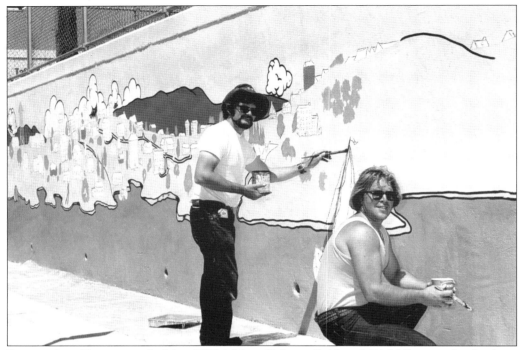

PUBLIC ART PROJECTS. In May 1973 Melvin Roberts (left) and Ed Miller put the finishing touches on a 136-foot-long mural at Lincoln Elementary School. The school's PTA donated the money for materials and the students, assisted by adult volunteers, painted the mural. In addition to murals like this one, Vallejo has numerous other public art projects. The downtown Marina Vista redevelopment area featured sculptures such as *The Genius* by Carl Milles, *Silent Company* by Gordon Newell and *Space* by Bella Tabak Feldman. (Courtesy of Vallejo *Times-Herald*.)

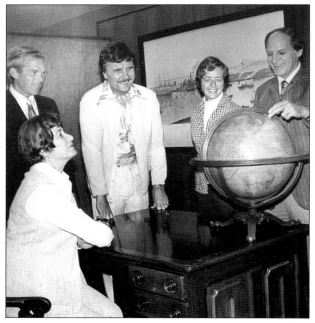

PRESERVING VALLEJO'S PAST. In 1974 the Vallejo Naval and Historical Museum was established to preserve the history of Vallejo and Mare Island. Museum volunteers began the work of converting Vallejo's historic old city hall into a museum, while temporary displays were set up around the community. One such display, shown here, was set up in the lobby of American Savings Bank. Pictured here, from left to right, are American Savings branch manager Charles Holland and museum board members Sue Lemmon, Richard Lemke, Rosella MacKennon, and Robert Keith.